TYPE 2 DIABETES DESSERT COOKBOOK

Scrumptious and Easy Recipes to Manage
Prediabetes and Type 2 Diabetes

Meg Schwartz

CONTENTS

Diabetic-friendly desserts that's both delicious and easy to make.

SUGAR-FREE APPLE CRUMBLE

Ingredients:

- 4 medium-sized apples, peeled and thinly sliced
- 1/4 cup granulated sugar substitute (such as Stevia or Splenda)
- 1 teaspoon ground cinnamon
- 1/2 cup all-purpose flour
- 1/2 cup old-fashioned oats
- 1/4 cup chopped walnuts
- 1/4 cup unsalted butter, melted

Instructions:

1. Preheat your oven to 350°F (175°C).
2. In a mixing bowl, combine the sliced apples, sugar substitute, and cinnamon. Stir well to coat the apples evenly. Then, transfer the mixture to an 8-inch square baking dish.
3. In a separate bowl, mix together the flour, oats, and chopped walnuts. Add the melted butter and stir until the mixture is crumbly and the ingredients are well combined.
4. Sprinkle the crumble mixture evenly over the top of the apple mixture.
5. Bake for 30-35 minutes, or until the topping is golden brown and the apples are tender.
6. Let the crumble cool for a few minutes before serving.

Enjoy this delicious sugar-free apple crumble warm, with a scoop of sugar-free vanilla ice cream or a dollop of whipped cream. It's the perfect dessert for anyone with a sweet tooth who's watching their sugar intake

LYCHEE COCONUT CHIA PUDDING
WITH LIME AND MINT

Ingredients:

- 1 can of lychees in syrup
- 1 can of full-fat coconut milk
- 1/2 cup of chia seeds
- 1 tsp of vanilla extract
- 1/4 tsp of cardamom powder
- 1/4 tsp of ground cinnamon
- 1/4 cup of unsweetened shredded coconut
- Juice of 1 lime
- Zest of 1 lime
- 1/4 cup of fresh mint leaves, chopped

Instructions:

1. Drain the lychees from the syrup and set aside.
2. In a mixing bowl, combine the coconut milk, chia seeds, vanilla extract, and cardamom powder, ground cinnamon, lime juice, and lime zest. Stir until well combined.
3. Transfer the mixture to a jar with a lid and refrigerate for at least 2 hours or overnight.
4. Once the pudding has set, takes it out of the fridge and stirs in the shredded coconut and chopped mint leaves.
5. To serve, spoon the pudding into bowls or glasses and top with the lychees.

This unique and flavorful twist on the classic lychee coconut chia pudding is sure to be a hit! The addition of lime and mint adds a refreshing and zesty kick to the creamy and sweet pudding. Enjoy!

MANGO AND LIME SORBET

Ingredients:

- 3 ripe mangoes, peeled and chopped
- 1/2 cup freshly squeezed lime juice
- 1/4 cup granulated sugar substitute (such as Stevia or Splenda)
- 1/4 cup water

Instructions:

1. In a blender or food processor, puree the chopped mangoes until smooth.
2. Add the lime juice, sugar substitute, and water to the blender and blend until well combined.
3. Pour the mixture into a shallow dish and freeze for 2-3 hours.
4. Use a fork to scrape the frozen mixture, breaking up any ice crystals that have formed.
5. Return the mixture to the freezer and repeat this process every 30 minutes until the sorbet is smooth and frozen.
6. Once the sorbet is frozen, transfer it to an airtight container and store it in the freezer until ready to serve.

This refreshing and fruity mango and lime sorbet is the perfect dessert for hot summer days. You can also experiment with other fruits, such as strawberries or raspberries, to create your own unique sorbet flavors. Enjoy!

.

LOW-CARB CHEESECAKE BITES

Dessert that's sure to satisfy your sweet tooth and impress your taste buds.

Ingredients:

For the crust:

- ½ cup almond flour
- ¼ cup coconut flour
- ¼ cup unsweetened shredded coconut

- 2 tbsp Swerve sweetener
- ¼ tsp salt
- ¼ cup melted coconut oil

For the filling:

- 8 oz cream cheese, softened
- ¼ cup Swerve sweetener
- 1 large egg

- 1 tsp vanilla extract
- ¼ tsp salt

Instructions:

1. Preheat the oven to 350°F and line a muffin tin with paper liners.
2. In a mixing bowl, combine almond flour, coconut flour, shredded coconut, Swerve sweetener, and salt. Add melted coconut oil and stir until well combined.
3. Divide the crust mixture among the muffin cups, pressing it firmly into the bottom to form a crust.
4. Bake the crusts for 8-10 minutes, or until lightly golden brown. Remove from the oven and set aside to cool.
5. In a separate mixing bowl, beat the cream cheese until smooth. Add Swerve sweetener, egg, vanilla extract, and salt. Beat until well combined and creamy.
6. Spoon the cream cheese mixture onto the cooled crusts, filling each cup almost to the top.
7. Bake the cheesecake bites for 18-20 minutes, or until set and slightly golden brown.
8. Remove from the oven and allow cooling to room temperature.

Serve and enjoy!

These low-carb cheesecake bites are a perfect diabetic-friendly dessert that won't spike your blood sugar levels. They are rich and creamy, with a deliciously crunchy crust. You can also add some fresh berries or a drizzle of sugar-free chocolate sauce to make them even more indulgent.

Enjoy your guilt-free sweet treat!

COCONUT FLOUR CHOCOLATE CHIP COOKIES

Ingredients:

- ½ cup coconut flour
- ¼ cup almond flour
- ¼ cup Swerve sweetener
- ¼ tsp salt
- ¼ tsp baking soda

- ¼ cup melted coconut oil
- 2 large eggs
- 1 tsp vanilla extract
- ¼ cup sugar-free chocolate chips

Instructions:

1. Preheat the oven to 350°F and line a baking sheet with parchment paper.
2. In a mixing bowl, combine coconut flour, almond flour, Swerve sweetener, salt, and baking soda.
3. Add melted coconut oil, eggs, and vanilla extract to the dry ingredients and stir until well combined.
4. Fold in the sugar-free chocolate chips.
5. Use a cookie scoop or spoon to drop the dough onto the prepared baking sheet, spacing them about 2 inches apart.
6. Use a fork to gently flatten the cookies.
7. Bake for 10-12 minutes, or until the edges are lightly golden brown.
8. Remove from the oven and let cool on the baking sheet for 5 minutes, then transfer to a wire rack to cool completely.

Serve and enjoy!

These coconut flour chocolate chip cookies are low in carbohydrates and sugar, and high in healthy fats and fiber. They are soft, chewy, and bursting with chocolate goodness. You can also add some chopped nuts or dried fruits to give them a crunchy texture and extra flavor.

Enjoy these guilt-free cookies as a dessert or snack, and don't forget to share them with your loved ones!

CHOCOLATE AVOCADO PUDDING

Ingredients:

- 2 ripe avocados, peeled and pitted
- 1/2 cup unsweetened cocoa powder
- 1/4 cup unsweetened almond milk
- 1/4 cup pure maple syrup
- 1 tsp vanilla extract
- pinch of salt

Instructions:

1. In a blender or food processor, blend the avocados until smooth.
2. Add in the cocoa powder, almond milk, maple syrup, vanilla extract, and salt. Blend until well combined and creamy.
3. Taste and adjust the sweetness as needed, adding more maple syrup if desired.
4. Transfer the pudding to a bowl or individual serving dishes, and chill in the refrigerator for at least 30 minutes before serving.

Note: For a thicker pudding, use less almond milk. For a thinner pudding, add more almond milk.

Enjoy this rich and creamy chocolate avocado pudding as a guilt-free diabetic-friendly dessert!

MIXED BERRY CRUMBLE

Ingredients:

- 2 cups mixed berries (fresh or frozen)
- 1/4 cup almond flour
- 1/4 cup rolled oats
- 1/4 cup chopped nuts (such as pecans or almonds)
- 2 tbsp pure maple syrup
- 2 tbsp coconut oil, melted
- 1 tsp cinnamon
- pinch of salt

Instructions:

1. Preheat the oven to 350°F (175°C).
2. In a mixing bowl, combine the mixed berries with 1 tbsp of the maple syrup. Toss to coat.
3. In another mixing bowl, combine the almond flour, rolled oats, chopped nuts, remaining 1 tbsp of maple syrup, melted coconut oil, cinnamon, and salt. Mix well to form a crumbly mixture.
4. In a baking dish, spread out the coated berries in an even layer.
5. Sprinkle the crumble mixture on top of the berries, covering them completely.
6. Bake in the preheated oven for 25-30 minutes, until the crumble is golden brown and the berries are bubbling.
7. Allow to cool for a few minutes before serving. Serve warm or at room temperature.

This mixed berry crumble is a sweet and satisfying dessert that won't spike your blood sugar levels.

COCONUT FLOUR PANCAKES
WITH BLUEBERRY SAUCE

Ingredients for Pancakes:

- 1/4 cup coconut flour
- 1/4 tsp baking powder
- 1/4 tsp cinnamon
- pinch of salt
- 2 eggs

- 1/4 cup unsweetened almond milk
- 1 tbsp coconut oil, melted
- 1 tsp vanilla extract
- 1 tbsp pure maple syrup (optional)

Ingredients for Blueberry Sauce:

- 1 cup fresh or frozen blueberries
- 1 tbsp pure maple syrup
- 1 tbsp water

- 1 tsp lemon juice
- pinch of salt

Instructions:

1. In a mixing bowl, whisk together the coconut flour, baking powder, cinnamon, and salt.
2. In another mixing bowl, whisk together the eggs, almond milk, melted coconut oil, vanilla extract, and optional maple syrup.
3. Add the dry ingredients to the wet ingredients, and whisk until smooth.
4. Heat a non-stick skillet over medium heat. Grease with coconut oil or cooking spray.
5. Using a 1/4 cup measuring cup, scoop the batter onto the skillet, forming small pancakes.
6. Cook for 2-3 minutes on each side, until golden brown and cooked through.
7. Remove from the skillet and repeat with the remaining batter.

For the Blueberry Sauce:

1. In a small saucepan, combine the blueberries, maple syrup, water, lemon juice, and salt.
2. Bring to a boil over medium-high heat.

3. Reduce the heat to medium-low and simmer for 5-7 minutes, until the blueberries have burst and the sauce has thickened.
4. Remove from the heat and let cool for a few minutes.

Serve the coconut flour pancakes warm with the blueberry sauce on top. Enjoy this delicious and healthy diabetic-friendly breakfast or dessert!

CHIA PUDDING WITH STRAWBERRIES AND ALMONDS

Ingredients:

- 1/4 cup chia seeds
- 1 cup unsweetened almond milk
- 1 tbsp pure maple syrup
- 1 tsp vanilla extract
- 1 cup sliced strawberries
- 1/4 cup sliced almonds

Instructions:

1. In a mixing bowl, whisk together the chia seeds, almond milk, maple syrup, and vanilla extract.
2. Let the mixture sit for 5 minutes, then whisk again to break up any clumps.
3. Cover the bowl and refrigerate for at least 2 hours or overnight, until the mixture thickens and forms a pudding-like consistency.
4. Once the chia pudding has set, spoon it into serving dishes.
5. Top each serving with sliced strawberries and sliced almonds.

This chia pudding with strawberries and almonds is a healthy and delicious diabetic-friendly dessert that's easy to make and packed with nutrients!

BAKED APPLES WITH CINNAMON AND WALNUTS

Ingredients:

- 4 medium-sized apples
- 1/4 cup chopped walnuts
- 2 tbsp pure maple syrup
- 1 tsp cinnamon
- 1/4 tsp nutmeg
- pinch of salt

Instructions:

1. Preheat the oven to 375°F (190°C).
2. Cut off the tops of the apples and use a spoon or melon baller to scoop out the cores, leaving a well in the center of each apple.
3. In a mixing bowl, combine the chopped walnuts, maple syrup, cinnamon, nutmeg, and salt.
4. Stuff each apple with the nut mixture, packing it tightly into the wells.
5. Place the stuffed apples in a baking dish and cover with foil.
6. Bake in the preheated oven for 20 minutes.
7. Remove the foil and bake for an additional 10-15 minutes, until the apples are tender and the nut mixture is golden brown.
8. Let cool for a few minutes before serving.

These baked apples with cinnamon and walnuts are a warm and cozy diabetic-friendly dessert that's perfect for a cold night

CHOCOLATE AVOCADO MOUSSE

Ingredients:

- 2 ripe avocados, pitted and peeled
- 1/4 cup unsweetened cocoa powder
- 1/4 cup pure maple syrup
- 1 tsp vanilla extract
- pinch of salt
- 1/4 cup unsweetened almond milk

Instructions:

1. In a food processor or blender, combine the avocados, cocoa powder, maple syrup, vanilla extract, and salt.
2. Pulse until the mixture is smooth and creamy, scraping down the sides as needed.
3. With the motor running, slowly add the almond milk and blend until the mixture is well combined and fluffy.
4. Spoon the mousse into serving dishes and refrigerate for at least 30 minutes to set.

This chocolate avocado mousse is a rich and decadent diabetic-friendly dessert that's packed with healthy fats and antioxidants.

Enjoy it as a guilt-free indulgence!

MIXED BERRY CRISP

Ingredients:

- 4 cups mixed berries (such as strawberries, blueberries, raspberries, and blackberries)
- 1 tbsp cornstarch
- 2 tbsp pure maple syrup
- 1 tsp lemon juice
- 1/2 cup rolled oats

- 1/4 cup almond flour
- 1/4 cup chopped walnuts
- 2 tbsp coconut oil, melted
- 2 tbsp pure maple syrup
- 1 tsp vanilla extract
- pinch of salt

Instructions:

1. Preheat the oven to 375°F (190°C).
2. In a mixing bowl, toss together the mixed berries, cornstarch, maple syrup, and lemon juice.
3. Transfer the berry mixture to a baking dish.
4. In another mixing bowl, combine the rolled oats, almond flour, chopped walnuts, melted coconut oil, maple syrup, vanilla extract, and salt.
5. Mix until the ingredients are well combined and crumbly.
6. Sprinkle the oat mixture over the berry mixture in the baking dish.
7. Bake in the preheated oven for 30-35 minutes, until the topping is golden brown and the berries are bubbling.
8. Let cool for a few minutes before serving.

This mixed berry crisp is a sweet and crunchy diabetic-friendly dessert that's perfect for showcasing the delicious flavors of fresh berries.

Enjoy it warm or cold, topped with a dollop of whipped cream or a scoop of vanilla ice cream, if desired.

COCONUT CHIA PUDDING WITH MANGO

Ingredients:

- 1/2 cup chia seeds
- 2 cups unsweetened coconut milk
- 1/4 cup pure maple syrup
- 1 tsp vanilla extract
- pinch of salt
- 1 ripe mango, peeled and diced

Instructions:

1. In a mixing bowl, whisk together the chia seeds, coconut milk, maple syrup, vanilla extract, and salt.
2. Let the mixture sit for 5-10 minutes, until the chia seeds absorb some of the liquid and the mixture thickens.
3. Whisk the mixture again to break up any clumps of chia seeds.
4. Cover the bowl and refrigerate for at least 1 hour, or overnight.
5. When ready to serve, divide the chia pudding into serving dishes and top with diced mango.

This coconut chia pudding with mango is a refreshing and healthy diabetic-friendly dessert that's perfect for a warm day. The combination of creamy coconut milk, nutty chia seeds, and juicy mango is simply irresistible!

APPLE CINNAMON
BAKED OATMEAL

Ingredients:

- 2 cups rolled oats
- 1 tsp baking powder
- 1 1/2 tsp ground cinnamon
- 1/4 tsp salt
- 2 cups unsweetened almond milk
- 1/4 cup pure maple syrup
- 1 tsp vanilla extract
- 1 medium apple, peeled and grated
- 1/4 cup chopped pecans

Instructions:

1. Preheat the oven to 375°F (190°C).
2. In a mixing bowl, combine the rolled oats, baking powder, cinnamon, and salt.
3. In another mixing bowl, whisk together the almond milk, maple syrup, and vanilla extract.
4. Pour the wet ingredients over the dry ingredients and mix until well combined.
5. Stir in the grated apple and chopped pecans.
6. Transfer the mixture to a baking dish and bake in the preheated oven for 35-40 minutes, until the top is golden brown and the oatmeal is set.
7. Let cool for a few minutes before serving.

This apple cinnamon baked oatmeal is a hearty and wholesome diabetic-friendly dessert that's perfect for a cozy breakfast or a sweet snack. The combination of warm spices, juicy apples, and crunchy pecans is sure to please your taste buds!

SPICED BAKED PEARS
WITH YOGURT AND HONEY

Ingredients:

- 4 ripe but firm pears
- 1 tsp ground cinnamon
- 1/4 tsp ground nutmeg
- 1/4 tsp ground ginger

- 1/4 cup honey
- 1/2 cup plain Greek yogurt
- 1 tbsp chopped pistachios

Instructions:

1. Preheat your oven to 375°F (190°C).
2. Cut each pear in half and scoop out the seeds with a spoon.
3. In a small bowl, mix together the cinnamon, nutmeg, and ginger.
4. Sprinkle the spice mixture over the pears, making sure to coat each one evenly.
5. Drizzle the honey over the pears, and then place them in a baking dish.
6. Bake the pears in the oven for 20-25 minutes, or until they are tender and golden brown.
7. While the pears are baking, mix together the Greek yogurt and a tablespoon of honey in a small bowl.
8. When the pears are done, let them cool for a few minutes, and then place them on a serving dish.
9. Top each pear half with a spoonful of the honey-yogurt mixture, and then sprinkle with chopped pistachios.

Serve warm and enjoy!

This is a healthy and satisfying way to indulge in a sweet treat without worrying about spiking your blood sugar. The combination of warm, spiced pears with cool, tangy yogurt and crunchy pistachios is sure to please any palate. Give it a try and let us know what you think!

MATCHA GREEN TEA COCONUT PUDDING

Ingredients:

- 2 cups unsweetened coconut milk
- 1/4 cup honey
- 1 tbsp matcha green tea powder
- 2 tsp gelatin powder
- 1/4 cup cold water
- 1/4 cup boiling water
- Fresh berries (optional, for serving)

Instructions:

1. In a medium saucepan, whisk together the coconut milk and honey over medium heat until well combined.
2. Add the matcha green tea powder and continue to whisk until the mixture is smooth and fully combined.
3. In a small bowl, sprinkle the gelatin powder over the cold water and let it sit for 5 minutes to soften.
4. Add the boiling water to the gelatin mixture and whisk until the gelatin has completely dissolved.
5. Pour the gelatin mixture into the coconut milk mixture and whisk until everything is fully combined.
6. Remove the saucepan from the heat and let the mixture cool for a few minutes.
7. Pour the mixture into individual dessert cups or ramekins and refrigerate for at least 2 hours, or until the pudding has set.
8. Before serving, garnish with fresh berries, if desired.

This is a delicious and unique way to enjoy the health benefits of matcha green tea in a sweet treat. The creamy coconut milk adds a rich and satisfying flavor, while the honey provides a natural sweetness that won't spike your blood sugar. Give it a try and enjoy a taste of Asia in your dessert!

MANGO STICKY RICE PUDDING

Ingredients:

- 1 cup glutinous rice (also known as sweet rice or sticky rice)
- 1 can (14 oz) light coconut milk
- 1/4 cup honey
- 1/4 tsp salt
- 2 ripe mangoes, peeled and sliced
- 1 tbsp toasted sesame seeds (optional, for garnish)

Instructions:

1. Rinse the glutinous rice in a fine-mesh strainer until the water runs clear. Then, soak the rice in cold water for at least 30 minutes.
2. In a medium saucepan, combine the coconut milk, honey, and salt over medium heat. Stir occasionally until the honey is fully dissolved.
3. Drain the soaked rice and add it to the saucepan with the coconut milk mixture. Stir to combine.
4. Bring the mixture to a boil, and then reduce the heat to low and cover the saucepan with a tight-fitting lid. Let the rice cook for 20-25 minutes, or until the liquid is fully absorbed and the rice is tender.
5. While the rice is cooking, slice the mangoes and set aside.
6. Once the rice is done, remove the saucepan from the heat and let it cool for a few minutes.
7. To serve, divide the rice pudding into individual bowls or plates, and top with sliced mangoes. Sprinkle with toasted sesame seeds, if desired.

This a sweet and satisfying way to enjoy the tropical flavors of mango and coconut in a dessert that's diabetes-friendly. The sticky rice provides a chewy texture that pairs perfectly with the creamy coconut milk and sweet mangoes. Give it a try and enjoy a taste of Southeast Asia in your own home!

BAKED LYCHEE AND ALMOND TARTS

Ingredients:

- 1 1/4 cups almond flour
- 1/4 cup coconut flour
- 1/4 cup honey
- 1/4 cup coconut oil, melted
- 1 tsp vanilla extract
- 1/2 tsp baking soda

- 1/4 tsp salt
- 1 can (20 oz) lychees in syrup, drained and pitted
- Whipped cream or Greek yogurt (optional, for serving)

Instructions:

1. Preheat your oven to 350°F (175°C).
2. In a large mixing bowl, combine the almond flour, coconut flour, honey, melted coconut oil, vanilla extract, baking soda, and salt. Mix well until a dough forms.
3. Divide the dough into 6 equal portions and press each portion into a 4-inch tart pan, making sure to cover the bottom and sides.
4. Arrange the drained and pitted lychees in the tart shells, pressing them gently into the dough.
5. Bake the tarts in the oven for 15-20 minutes, or until the crust is golden brown and the filling is hot and bubbly.
6. Remove the tarts from the oven and let them cool for a few minutes before serving.

NOTE: If desired, top each tart with a dollop of whipped cream or Greek yogurt before serving.

This is a delicious and unique way to enjoy the sweet and exotic flavor of lychees in a diabetes-friendly dessert. The almond flour and coconut oil provide a healthy source of fats and fiber, while the natural sweetness of honey adds a touch of indulgence. Give it a try and enjoy a taste of Asia in your dessert!

CHAI SPICED POACHED PEARS

Ingredients:

- 4 ripe pears, peeled and cored
- 2 cups water
- 1 cup unsweetened almond milk
- 2 black tea bags
- 1 cinnamon stick
- 4 cardamom pods, crushed
- 1 star anise
- 1/4 cup honey
- 1 tsp vanilla extract

Instructions:

1. In a large saucepan, combine the water, almond milk, black tea bags, cinnamon stick, crushed cardamom pods, star anise, honey, and vanilla extract. Stir to combine.
2. Bring the mixture to a boil over medium-high heat, stirring occasionally.
3. Reduce the heat to low and add the peeled and cored pears to the saucepan. Make sure the pears are fully submerged in the liquid.
4. Cover the saucepan with a lid and let the pears simmer for 15-20 minutes, or until they are tender.
5. Remove the saucepan from the heat and let the pears cool in the poaching liquid for at least 10 minutes.
6. Once the pears are cool, remove them from the poaching liquid and place them on a serving platter.
7. Strain the poaching liquid through a fine-mesh strainer and discard the solids. Return the liquid to the saucepan and bring it to a boil over medium-high heat.
8. Reduce the heat to low and let the liquid simmer for 10-15 minutes, or until it has reduced and thickened into a syrup.
9. Pour the syrup over the poached pears and serve immediately.

This is a flavorful and unique way to enjoy pears in a diabetes-friendly dessert. The chai spices provide a warm and comforting flavor, while the almond milk and honey add a touch of sweetness without spiking your blood sugar. Give it a try and enjoy a taste of India in your dessert!

MATCHA GREEN TEA AND ALMOND BUTTER COOKIES

Ingredients:

- 1 cup almond flour
- 1/4 cup unsweetened matcha green tea powder
- 1/4 cup almond butter
- 1/4 cup coconut oil, melted
- 1/4 cup honey
- 1 tsp vanilla extract
- 1/2 tsp baking soda
- 1/4 tsp salt

Instructions:

1. Preheat your oven to 350°F (175°C).
2. In a large mixing bowl, combine the almond flour, matcha powder, almond butter, melted coconut oil, honey, vanilla extract, baking soda, and salt. Mix well until a dough forms.
3. Roll the dough into small balls, about 1 inch in diameter.
4. Place the dough balls on a baking sheet lined with parchment paper. Use a fork to gently press down on each ball to flatten it slightly.
5. Bake the cookies in the oven for 10-12 minutes, or until they are golden brown and slightly firm to the touch.
6. Remove the cookies from the oven and let them cool on the baking sheet for a few minutes before transferring them to a wire rack to cool completely.

Serve the cookies immediately, or store them in an airtight container for up to a week.

This is a unique and delicious way to enjoy the health benefits of matcha green tea in a diabetes-friendly dessert. The almond flour and almond butter provide a healthy source of fats and protein, while the natural sweetness of honey adds a touch of indulgence. Give it a try and enjoy a taste of Japan in your dessert!

MANGO COCONUT CHIA PUDDING

Ingredients:

- 1/2 cup chia seeds
- 2 cups unsweetened coconut milk
- 1 ripe mango, peeled and diced
- 2 tbsp honey
- 1 tsp vanilla extract
- 1/4 cup unsweetened shredded coconut

Instructions:

1. In a mixing bowl, combine the chia seeds, coconut milk, honey, and vanilla extract. Mix well until everything is evenly combined.
2. Cover the bowl with plastic wrap and refrigerate for at least 4 hours or overnight, to allow the chia seeds to absorb the liquid and thicken.
3. Once the chia pudding has thickened, divide it evenly between 4 serving dishes.
4. Top each serving with diced mango and a sprinkle of shredded coconut.
5. Serve the pudding immediately or store it in the refrigerator for up to 2 days.

This is a refreshing and unique way to enjoy the tropical flavors of mango and coconut in a diabetes-friendly dessert. The chia seeds provide a healthy source of fiber and omega-3 fatty acids, while the natural sweetness of honey adds a touch of indulgence without spiking your blood sugar. Give it a try and enjoy a taste of the tropics in your dessert!

MOCHA ICE CREAM

Ingredients:

- 1 cup mochiko (sweet rice flour)
- 1/4 cup cornstarch
- 1/4 cup honey
- 1/4 cup coconut oil, melted
- 1/2 cup water
- 1 pint sugar-free ice cream, any flavor

Instructions:

1. Preheat your oven to 350°F (175°C).
2. In a mixing bowl, combine the mochiko, cornstarch, honey, melted coconut oil, and water. Mix well until a dough forms.
3. Divide the dough into 12 equal-sized pieces and roll each piece into a ball.
4. Flatten each ball into a disc shape and place a small scoop of ice cream in the center.
5. Carefully pinch the edges of the mochi dough together around the ice cream to create a sealed ball.
6. Place the mochi balls on a baking sheet lined with parchment paper and bake in the oven for 10-12 minutes, or until the mochi is slightly firm and the edges are golden brown.
7. Remove the mochi balls from the oven and let them cool for a few minutes before serving.

This is a unique and delicious way to enjoy mochi and ice cream in a diabetes-friendly dessert. The mochiko flour provides gluten-free and low-glycemic alternative to regular flour, while the honey and coconut oil add a touch of sweetness and healthy fats. Give it a try and enjoy a taste of Japan in your dessert!

COCONUT MILK PANNA COTTA WITH LYCHEE COMPOTE

Ingredients:

- 1 can (13.5 oz) full-fat coconut milk
- 1/2 cup unsweetened almond milk
- 1/4 cup honey
- 2 tsp vanilla extract
- 1 tbsp unflavored gelatin

- 1 can (20 oz) lychee fruit in syrup, drained
- 1/4 cup water
- 1 tbsp lime juice

Instructions:

1. In a medium saucepan, heat the coconut milk, almond milk, honey, and vanilla extract over medium heat until it begins to simmer.
2. Remove the saucepan from the heat and sprinkle the gelatin over the surface of the liquid. Stir gently until the gelatin is completely dissolved.
3. Divide the mixture evenly among 4 ramekins or dessert cups.
4. Chill the panna cotta in the refrigerator for at least 4 hours or until set.
5. In a separate saucepan, combine the lychee fruit, water, and lime juice. Heat the mixture over medium heat, stirring occasionally, until it comes to a simmer.
6. Reduce the heat to low and let the lychee mixture simmer for 10-15 minutes, or until it thickens into a compote-like consistency.
7. Remove the lychee compote from the heat and let it cool to room temperature.
8. To serve, spoon a dollop of the lychee compote over each panna cotta.

This is a unique and flavorful way to enjoy a classic Italian dessert with an Asian twist. The coconut milk provides a rich and creamy base, while the lychee fruit adds a touch of sweetness and tropical flavor. Give it a try and impress your guests with this delicious and diabetes-friendly dessert!

CHIA SEED PUDDING WITH MANGO, STRAWBERRY, AND COCONUT

Ingredients:

- 1/4 cup chia seeds
- 1 cup unsweetened almond milk
- 1/4 cup unsweetened shredded coconut
- 2 tbsp honey
- 1 tsp vanilla extract
- 1 ripe mango, peeled and diced
- 1/2 cup fresh strawberries, sliced
- 1 tbsp sliced almonds (optional)

Instructions:

1. In a mixing bowl, combine the chia seeds, almond milk, shredded coconut, honey, and vanilla extract. Mix well until fully combined.
2. Cover the bowl with plastic wrap and refrigerate for at least 2 hours or overnight to allow the chia seeds to absorb the liquid and thicken.
3. Once the chia seed mixture has thickened, remove it from the refrigerator and stir in the diced mango and sliced strawberries.
4. Divide the pudding evenly into 4 serving bowls and top with sliced almonds, if desired.

Nutrient information (per serving):

- Calories: 190
- Total Fat: 10g
- Saturated Fat: 4g
- Trans Fat: 0g
- Cholesterol: 0mg
- Sodium: 60mg
- Total Carbohydrates: 25g
- Dietary Fiber: 8g
- Sugars: 14g
- Protein: 4g

This is a delicious and diabetes-friendly way to enjoy a sweet treat that is also packed with nutrients. The chia seeds provide a good source of fiber and omega-3 fatty acids, while the mango and strawberries add vitamins and antioxidants. The almonds provide a healthy dose of protein and healthy fats. Give it a try and enjoy a guilt-free dessert!

DIABETIC-FRIENDLY ZARDA
(SWEET SAFFRON RICE)

Ingredients:

- 1 cup basmati rice
- 2 cups water
- 1/4 tsp saffron threads
- 1 cinnamon stick
- 2 green cardamom pods, crushed

- 1/4 cup raisins
- 1/4 cup chopped unsalted pistachios
- 1/4 cup chopped unsalted almonds
- 1/4 cup honey

Instructions:

1. Rinse the rice thoroughly in cold water until the water runs clear.
2. In a medium saucepan, bring the water to a boil. Add the rinsed rice, saffron threads, cinnamon stick, and cardamom pods. Stir once to combine.
3. Reduce the heat to low, cover the saucepan with a tight-fitting lid, and simmer for 18-20 minutes, or until the rice is fully cooked and the water has been absorbed.
4. Once the rice is cooked, remove the saucepan from the heat and fluff the rice with a fork.
5. Add the raisins, chopped pistachios, chopped almonds, and honey to the rice. Stir gently to combine.
6. Cover the saucepan again and let the rice sit for 5-10 minutes to allow the flavors to meld.
7. Once the rice has rested, remove the cinnamon stick and cardamom pods.
8. Serve the Zarda warm or at room temperature, garnished with additional chopped nuts if desired.

This uses honey as a natural sweetener instead of sugar, and includes healthy nuts and spices for added flavor and nutrients. Enjoy this diabetic-friendly version of Zarda as a delicious and guilt-free dessert!

DIABETIC-FRIENDLY CARROT HALWA

Ingredients:

- 2 cups grated carrots
- 1/4 cup unsweetened almond milk
- 1/4 cup chopped unsalted almonds
- 1/4 cup chopped unsalted cashews
- 1/4 cup raisins
- 2 tbsp ghee (clarified butter)
- 1/2 tsp ground cardamom
- 1/4 tsp ground cinnamon
- 1/4 cup honey

Instructions:

1. In a large non-stick skillet, heat the ghee over medium heat.
2. Add the grated carrots to the skillet and cook, stirring occasionally, for 5-7 minutes, or until the carrots are slightly softened.
3. Add the almond milk to the skillet and continue to cook the carrots for another 10-15 minutes, or until they are fully cooked and tender.
4. Stir in the chopped almonds, chopped cashews, raisins, cardamom, and cinnamon. Cook for an additional 5 minutes, stirring occasionally.
5. Once the nuts and spices have been fully incorporated, remove the skillet from the heat and stir in the honey.
6. Let the Halwa cool for a few minutes before serving, garnished with additional chopped nuts if desired.

This uses honey as a natural sweetener instead of sugar and includes healthy nuts and spices for added flavor and nutrients. Enjoy this diabetic-friendly version of Halwa as a delicious and guilt-free dessert!

DIABETIC-FRIENDLY
VANILLA ICE CREAM

Ingredients:

- 2 cans of full-fat coconut milk
- 1/2 cup heavy cream
- 1/4 cup honey or maple syrup
- 1 tsp pure vanilla extract
- Pinch of salt

Instructions:

1. In a large mixing bowl, whisk together the coconut milk, heavy cream, honeys or maple syrup, vanilla extract, and salt until well combined.
2. Pour the mixture into an ice cream maker and churn according to the manufacturer's instructions until the ice cream is thick and creamy.
3. Transfer the ice cream to a container and freeze for at least 4 hours or until firm.
4. Let the ice cream sit at room temperature for 5-10 minutes before scooping and serving.

This uses coconut milk instead of cow's milk and a natural sweetener instead of sugar to make it diabetic-friendly. Enjoy this delicious and guilt-free vanilla ice cream!

CHOCOLATE AVOCADO MOUSSE

Ingredients:

- 1 ripe avocado, peeled and pitted
- 1/4 cup unsweetened cocoa powder
- 1/4 cup almond milk
- 2 tablespoons honey
- 1/2 teaspoon vanilla extract
- Pinch of salt

Instructions:

1. Place the avocado, cocoa powder, almond milk, honey, vanilla extract, and salt in a blender or food processor.
2. Blend until smooth and creamy, scraping down the sides of the blender or food processor as needed.
3. Divide the mousse into 4 small dessert cups.
4. Chill in the refrigerator for at least 30 minutes before serving.

SERVE AND ENJOY

CINNAMON CHURRO BITES

Ingredients:

- 1 cup almond flour
- 1/4 cup coconut flour
- 1/4 cup granulated erythritol sweetener
- 1/4 cup butter, melted
- 1 egg
- 1/2 teaspoon baking powder
- 1/2 teaspoon ground cinnamon
- Pinch of salt
- Coconut oil or cooking spray for greasing

Instructions:

1. Preheat the oven to 350°F (175°C). Grease a mini muffin tin with coconut oil or cooking spray.
2. In a large bowl, whisk together the almond flour, coconut flour, erythritol sweetener, baking powder, cinnamon, and salt.
3. Add the melted butter and egg to the bowl and stir until a thick batter forms.
4. Using a cookie scoop or spoon, portion the batter into the prepared mini muffin tin.
5. Bake for 10-12 minutes or until golden brown and cooked through.
6. Allow the churro bites to cool in the muffin tin for a few minutes before removing them and rolling them in additional cinnamon.

SERVE AND ENJOY TOGETHER!

COCONUT FLAN

Ingredients:

- 1 can full-fat coconut milk
- 3 eggs
- 1/2 cup granulated erythritol sweetener
- 1/2 teaspoon vanilla extract
- Pinch of salt
- Shredded coconut for topping

Instructions:

1. Preheat the oven to 350°F (175°C).
2. In a large bowl, whisk together the coconut milk, eggs, erythritol sweetener, vanilla extract, and salt.
3. Pour the mixture into four 6-ounce ramekins.
4. Place the ramekins in a baking dish and fill the dish with enough water to come halfway up the sides of the ramekins.
5. Bake for 40-45 minutes or until the flan is set and jiggles slightly when shaken.
6. Remove the ramekins from the baking dish and let them cool to room temperature before refrigerating for at least 1 hour.
7. Before serving, top each flan with shredded coconut.

ENJOY!

MEXICAN SPICED CHOCOLATE PUDDING

Ingredients:

- 2 cups unsweetened almond milk
- 1/4 cup cornstarch
- 1/4 cup unsweetened cocoa powder
- 1/4 cup granulated erythritol sweetener
- 1/2 teaspoon ground cinnamon
- 1/4 teaspoon ground nutmeg
- Pinch of salt
- 1 teaspoon vanilla extract

Instructions:

1. In a medium saucepan, whisk together the almond milk, cornstarch, cocoa powder, erythritol sweetener, cinnamon, nutmeg, and salt until smooth.
2. Place the saucepan over medium heat and cook, whisking constantly, until the mixture thickens and comes to a boil.
3. Remove the saucepan from the heat and stir in the vanilla extract.
4. Pour the pudding into 4 small dessert cups or ramekins.
5. Chill in the refrigerator for at least 30 minutes before serving.
6. Optional: top the pudding with a dollop of whipped cream or sprinkle with additional cinnamon for extra flavor.

Note: You can adjust the sweetness level to your preference by adding more or less erythritol sweetener. You can also use other spices like chili powder or cayenne pepper to add a spicy kick to the pudding.

COCONUT LIME POPSICLES

Ingredients:

- 1 can full-fat coconut milk
- 1/4 cup granulated erythritol sweetener
- 1/4 cup lime juice
- 1 tablespoon lime zest
- 1/4 teaspoon vanilla extract
- Pinch of salt

Instructions:

1. In a large bowl, whisk together the coconut milk, erythritol sweetener, lime juice, lime zest, vanilla extract, and salt until well combined.
2. Pour the mixture into popsicle molds, leaving a little bit of space at the top for expansion.
3. Insert popsicle sticks into the molds and freeze for at least 4 hours or until completely frozen.
4. To remove the popsicles from the molds, run them under warm water for a few seconds to loosen them.
5. Serve and enjoy the refreshing coconut lime flavor.

Optional: You can add shredded coconut or chopped nuts to the popsicle mixture for added texture and crunch. You can also use other citrus fruits like lemon or orange instead of lime.

STRAWBERRY BASIL SORBET

Ingredients:

- 2 cups fresh strawberries, hulled and halved
- 1/4 cup granulated erythritol sweetener
- 1/4 cup water
- 1/4 cup fresh basil leaves, chopped
- 1 tablespoon lime juice

Instructions:

1. In a medium saucepan, combine the strawberries, erythritol sweetener, and water.
2. Bring the mixture to a simmer over medium heat, stirring occasionally, until the strawberries are soft and the sweetener has dissolved.
3. Remove the saucepan from the heat and stir in the chopped basil leaves and lime juice.
4. Allow the mixture to cool to room temperature.
5. Transfer the mixture to a blender or food processor and blend until smooth.
6. Pour the mixture into a freezer-safe container and freeze for 4-6 hours or until firm.
7. Remove the container from the freezer and let the sorbet sit at room temperature for a few minutes before scooping and serving.

Optional: You can use other fruits like raspberries or blackberries instead of strawberries. You can also substitute the basil with mint or rosemary for a different flavor profile.

MEXICAN COFFEE FLAN

Ingredients:

- 1/2 cup granulated erythritol sweetener
- 1/4 cup water
- 2 cups unsweetened almond milk
- 2 teaspoons instant coffee
- 1/2 teaspoon ground cinnamon
- 1 teaspoon vanilla extract
- 4 large eggs
- 1/4 teaspoon salt

Instructions:

1. Preheat the oven to 350°F.
2. In a small saucepan, combine the erythritol sweetener and water. Cook over medium heat until the sweetener has dissolved and the mixture turns golden brown, about 5 minutes.
3. Pour the caramel into a 9-inch round baking dish and swirl to coat the bottom evenly. Set aside.
4. In a medium saucepan, heat the almond milk over medium heat until it comes to a simmer.
5. Whisk in the instant coffee, cinnamon, and vanilla extract until well combined.
6. In a separate bowl, whisk together the eggs and salt.
7. Slowly pour the hot almond milk mixture into the bowl with the eggs, whisking constantly.
8. Pour the mixture into the prepared baking dish.
9. Place the baking dish in a larger baking pan and fill the larger pan with enough hot water to come up to the level of the flan mixture.
10. Bake for 50-55 minutes or until the edges are set but the center is still jiggly.
11. Remove the baking dish from the water bath and let it cool to room temperature.
12. Cover and refrigerate for at least 2 hours or overnight.
13. To serve, run a knife around the edge of the flan to loosen it. Place a plate on top of the dish and invert the flan onto the plate.

14. Slice and serve chilled.

Optional: You can sprinkle some ground cinnamon or cocoa powder on top for extra flavor and presentation.

CINNAMON APPLE EMPANADAS

Ingredients:

For the filling:

- 2 medium apples, peeled and diced
- 1/4 cup granulated erythritol sweetener
- 1/2 teaspoon ground cinnamon
- 1 tablespoon unsalted butter
- 1 tablespoon water

For the dough:

- 1 cup almond flour
- 1/4 cup coconut flour
- 1/4 cup granulated erythritol sweetener
- 1/4 teaspoon baking powder
- 1/4 teaspoon salt
- 4 tablespoons unsalted butter, chilled and cut into small pieces
- 1 egg, beaten

Instructions:

1. Preheat the oven to 375°F and line a baking sheet with parchment paper.
2. To make the filling, combine the diced apples, erythritol sweetener, ground cinnamon, butter, and water in a medium saucepan.
3. Cook over medium heat for 8-10 minutes or until the apples are soft and the mixture has thickened.
4. Remove from heat and set aside to cool.
5. To make the dough, whisk together the almond flour, coconut flour, erythritol sweetener, baking powder, and salt in a large bowl.
6. Add the chilled butter pieces and use a pastry cutter or your hands to mix until the mixture resembles coarse sand.
7. Add the beaten egg and stir until the dough comes together in a ball.
8. On a lightly floured surface, roll the dough out to about 1/4 inch thickness.
9. Use a circular cookie cutter or cup to cut out circles of dough.
10. Spoon a small amount of the apple filling onto one half of each dough circle.

11. Fold the other half of the dough over the filling and use a fork to press the edges together to seal.

12. Place the empanadas on the prepared baking sheet.

13. Bake for 12-15 minutes or until lightly golden brown.

14. Remove from the oven and let cool for a few minutes before serving.

Optional: You can brush the empanadas with a beaten egg before baking for a shiny and crispy finish. You can also add a pinch of nutmeg or ginger to the apple filling for added flavor.

LIME AND COCONUT SORBET

Ingredients:

- 1 can (13.5 oz) unsweetened coconut milk
- 1/2 cup granulated erythritol sweetener
- 1/2 cup water
- 1/2 cup fresh lime juice (about 4 limes)
- 1 tablespoon lime zest

Instructions:

1. In a medium saucepan, combine the coconut milk, erythritol sweetener, and water. Cook over medium heat, stirring constantly, until the sweetener has dissolved.
2. Remove from heat and let cool to room temperature.
3. Stir in the lime juice and lime zest.
4. Transfer the mixture to a blender and blend until smooth.
5. Pour the mixture into an ice cream maker and churn according to the manufacturer's instructions.
6. Transfer the sorbet to a freezer-safe container and freeze for at least 4 hours or until firm.
7. To serve, let the sorbet sit at room temperature for a few minutes to soften before scooping.

Optional: You can garnish with some toasted coconut flakes or a slice of lime for added flavor and presentation. You can also substitute the lime juice and zest with other citrus fruits such as lemon or grapefruit for a different variation of the sorbet.

MEXICAN CHOCOLATE CHIA PUDDING

Ingredients:

- 1 can (13.5 oz) unsweetened coconut milk
- 1/4 cup chia seeds
- 1/4 cup unsweetened cocoa powder
- 1/4 cup granulated erythritol sweetener
- 1/2 teaspoon ground cinnamon
- 1/4 teaspoon ground nutmeg
- 1/4 teaspoon salt
- 1/2 teaspoon vanilla extract

Instructions:

1. In a large mixing bowl, whisk together the coconut milk, chia seeds, cocoa powder, erythritol sweetener, cinnamon, nutmeg, salt, and vanilla extract until well combined.
2. Cover the bowl with plastic wrap and refrigerate for at least 2 hours or overnight.
3. Before serving, stir the pudding well and divide into serving bowls.
4. Garnish with fresh berries or chopped nuts, if desired.

Optional: For a spicier twist, you can add a pinch of cayenne pepper or chili powder to the mixture. You can also experiment with different types of milk such as almond milk or soy milk for a different flavor profile.

LOW-CARB TIRAMISU

Ingredients:

- 8 ounces of mascarpone cheese
- 2/3 cup of heavy cream
- 1 teaspoon of vanilla extract
- 1/4 cup of granulated sugar substitute
- 1 package of ladyfingers
- 1/2 cup of strong brewed coffee
- 1 tablespoon of unsweetened cocoa powder

Instructions:

1. In a large mixing bowl, beat the mascarpone cheese until it is smooth and creamy.
2. Add in the heavy cream, vanilla extract and sugar substitute and beat until the mixture is thick and creamy.
3. Dip the ladyfingers into the coffee and arrange them in the bottom of a 9x9 inch baking dish.
4. Pour half of the mascarpone mixture over the ladyfingers and spread it out evenly.
5. Repeat with another layer of dipped ladyfingers and the remaining mascarpone mixture.
6. Sift the cocoa powder over the top of the tiramisu.
7. Cover the dish with plastic wrap and refrigerate for at least 2 hours before serving.

ENJOY!

ALMOND FLOUR CANNOLI SHELLS

Ingredients:

- 1 1/2 cups of almond flour
- 1/4 cup of granulated sugar substitute
- 1/4 teaspoon of salt
- 1/4 cup of unsalted butter, melted
- 1/2 teaspoon of vanilla extract
- 1 egg white
- 1/4 cup of chopped pistachios (optional)

Instructions:

1. Preheat your oven to 350°F.
2. In a large mixing bowl, whisk together the almond flour, sugar substitute, and salt.
3. Add in the melted butter and vanilla extract and stir until the mixture forms a dough.
4. Roll out the dough to 1/4 inch thickness and use a cannoli mold to cut out 4 inch circles.
5. Wrap each circle around the cannoli mold and brush the edges with egg white to seal them.
6. Bake the cannoli shells for 12-15 minutes, or until they are golden brown.
7. Let the shells cool completely before removing them from the molds.
8. Sprinkle the chopped pistachios over the ends of the cannoli shells before filling them.

SERVE WITH SMILE!

FLOURLESS CHOCOLATE CAKE

Ingredients:

- 8 ounces of dark chocolate, chopped
- 1/2 cup of unsalted butter, cut into small pieces
- 1/2 cup of granulated sugar substitute
- 4 large eggs
- 1 teaspoon of vanilla extract
- 1/4 teaspoon of salt

Instructions:

1. Preheat your oven to 350°F.
2. Grease an 8 inch cake pan and line the bottom with parchment paper.
3. In a large heatproof bowl, melt the chocolate and butter together in the microwave or over a double boiler.
4. Stir in the sugar substitute, eggs, vanilla extract, and salt until the mixture is smooth and well combined.
5. Pour the batter into the prepared cake pan and smooth out the top.
6. Bake the cake for 25-30 minutes, or until the edges are set but the center is still slightly jiggly.
7. Let the cake cool in the pan for 10 minutes before removing it from the pan and transferring it to a wire rack to cool completely.
8. Serve the cake with whipped cream or fresh berries, if desired.

Enjoy this delicious and unique Italian diabetic dessert!

RICOTTA CHEESECAKE

Ingredients:

- 2 cups of part-skim ricotta cheese
- 1/2 cup of granulated sugar substitute
- 1/4 cup of almond flour
- 2 tablespoons of unsalted butter, melted
- 1/4 teaspoon of salt
- 1/4 teaspoon of cinnamon
- 3 large eggs
- 1/4 cup of unsweetened cocoa powder

Instructions:

1. Preheat your oven to 350°F.
2. Grease a 9 inch spring form pan and line the bottom with parchment paper.
3. In a large mixing bowl, whisk together the ricotta cheese, sugar substitute, almond flour, melted butter, salt, and cinnamon until well combined.
4. Add in the eggs one at a time, whisking well after each addition.
5. Pour half of the cheesecake batter into the prepared pan.
6. Sift the cocoa powder over the remaining batter and whisk until well combined.
7. Pour the chocolate batter over the plain batter in the pan.
8. Bake the cheesecake for 45-50 minutes, or until the edges are set but the center is still slightly jiggly.
9. Let the cheesecake cool in the pan for 10 minutes before removing it from the pan and transferring it to a wire rack to cool completely.

Chill the cheesecake in the refrigerator for at least 2 hours before serving. Enjoy!

PEANUT BUTTER BANANA OATMEAL COOKIES

Ingredients:

- 2 ripe bananas, mashed
- 1/2 cup peanut butter
- 1/4 cup honey
- 1 egg
- 1 teaspoon vanilla extract
- 1/2 teaspoon baking soda
- 1/4 teaspoon salt
- 2 cups rolled oats

Directions:

1. Preheat the oven to 350°F (175°C) and line a baking sheet with parchment paper.
2. In a large bowl, mix together the mashed bananas, peanut butter, honey, egg, and vanilla extract.
3. Add the baking soda and salt, and mix well.
4. Stir in the rolled oats until well combined.
5. Using a cookie scoop or spoon, drop the dough onto the prepared baking sheet, spacing the cookies about 2 inches apart.
6. Bake for 12-15 minutes, or until the edges are lightly browned.
7. Let the cookies cool on the baking sheet for a few minutes before transferring them to a wire rack to cool completely. Serve and eat.

STICKY TOFFEE PUDDING

Ingredients:

- 1 cup pitted dates, chopped
- 1 cup boiling water
- 1/4 cup coconut oil
- 1/4 cup honey
- 2 large eggs
- 1 teaspoon vanilla extract
- 1 cup almond flour
- 1 teaspoon baking powder
- 1/2 teaspoon ground cinnamon
- 1/4 teaspoon salt
- For the toffee sauce:
- 1/4 cup coconut oil
- 1/4 cup honey
- 1/2 cup full-fat coconut milk

Directions:

1. Preheat the oven to 350°F (175°C).
2. In a bowl, pour the boiling water over the chopped dates and let them soak for 10 minutes.
3. In another bowl, cream together the coconut oil and honey. Add the eggs and vanilla extract and beat until well combined.
4. In a separate bowl, mix together the almond flour, baking powder, cinnamon, and salt.
5. Add the dry ingredients to the wet ingredients and mix until just combined. Stir in the soaked dates and their liquid.
6. Pour the batter into a greased 8-inch square baking dish. Bake for 30-35 minutes, or until a toothpick inserted into the center comes out clean.
7. While the pudding is baking, prepare the toffee sauce by heating the coconut oil, honey, and coconut milk in a saucepan over medium heat. Cook for 5-7 minutes, stirring constantly, until the sauce thickens and becomes sticky.
8. Serve the warm pudding with the toffee sauce drizzled over the top.

MINT AND LEMON SORBET

Ingredients:

- 1 cup fresh lemon juice
- 2 tbsp honey
- 1/4 cup fresh mint leaves, chopped
- 2 cups water

Instructions:

1. In a medium saucepan, mix together the lemon juice, honey, and chopped mint leaves.
2. Bring the mixture to a boil over medium heat, stirring occasionally.
3. Reduce the heat to low and let the mixture simmer for 5-10 minutes, until the honey has dissolved and the mint leaves have infused the mixture.
4. Remove the mixture from the heat and let it cool to room temperature.
5. Once cooled, strain the mixture through a fine-mesh sieve to remove the mint leaves.
6. Mix in the water and pour the mixture into a freezer-safe container.
7. Freeze the mixture for 2-3 hours, or until it's mostly frozen.
8. Using a fork, scrape the mixture to break up any ice crystals and return it to the freezer.
9. Repeat this process every 30 minutes for 2-3 hours, until the sorbet is completely frozen and has a smooth texture.
10. Serve the sorbet immediately, garnished with fresh mint leaves, if desired.

This mint and lemon sorbet is a refreshing and healthy dessert option that's perfect for those with diabetes. The use of fresh lemon juice provides a good source of vitamin C and antioxidants, while the addition of honey instead of sugar helps to keep the glycemic index low. The use of fresh mint provides a bright and refreshing flavor, while the freezing process creates a smooth and creamy texture. Enjoy this sorbet as a light and guilt-free dessert option that's perfect for cooling off on a hot day.

SUGAR-FREE CHOCOLATE MOUSSE

Ingredients:

- 1 cup heavy cream
- 1/4 cup unsweetened cocoa powder
- 1/4 cup granulated sugar substitute (such as erythritol or stevia)
- 1/2 tsp vanilla extract
- Pinch of salt

Instructions:

1. In a medium-sized mixing bowl, combine the heavy cream, cocoa powder, sugar substitute, vanilla extract, and salt.
2. Using an electric mixer beat the mixture until it becomes smooth and thick.
3. Spoon the mousse into individual serving dishes, such as ramekins or small bowls.
4. Refrigerate the mousse for at least one hour before serving.
5. When you're ready to serve the mousse, you can garnish it with sugar-free whipped cream and fresh berries, if desired.

This sugar-free chocolate mousse is perfect for people with diabetes, as it contains no added sugar and is low in carbohydrates. The heavy cream provides a rich and creamy texture, while the cocoa powder adds a deep chocolate flavor. The sugar substitute gives the mousse its sweetness without spiking blood sugar levels. Enjoy!

YOGURT AND WALNUT TART

Ingredients:

For the crust:

- 1 cup almond flour
- 1/4 cup unsalted butter, melted
- 1/4 cup honey
- 1/4 tsp salt

For the filling:

- 2 cups plain Greek yogurt
- 1/4 cup honey
- 1/2 cup chopped walnuts
- 1/2 tsp ground cinnamon
- 1/4 tsp ground cardamom
- 1/4 tsp vanilla extract

Instructions:

1. Preheat your oven to 350°F (175°C).
2. In a medium bowl, combine the almond flour, melted butter, honey, and salt to make the crust.
3. Press the crust mixture into a 9-inch tart pan, spreading it evenly across the bottom and up the sides of the pan.
4. Bake the crust for 10-12 minutes, or until it is lightly golden brown.
5. Remove the crust from the oven and let it cool to room temperature.
6. In a large bowl, mix the yogurt, honey, walnuts, cinnamon, cardamom, and vanilla extract to make the filling.
7. Pour the filling into the cooled crust, spreading it evenly across the crust.
8. Bake the tart for 30-35 minutes, or until the filling is set and the edges of the crust are golden brown.
9. Remove the tart from the oven and let it cool to room temperature.
10. Once cooled, slice the tart and serve.

This yogurt and walnut tart is a delicious and diabetes-friendly dessert option that's perfect for those who want to enjoy a sweet treat without worrying about their blood sugar levels.

The use of almond flour in the crust helps to keep the carbohydrates low, while the Greek yogurt provides a good source of protein. The addition of honey, walnuts, cinnamon, and cardamom provide natural sweetness and flavor without spiking blood sugar levels. This tart is perfect for serving as a dessert after a Turkish-inspired meal or for enjoying as a snack throughout the day.

TURKISH APRICOT
AND ALMOND BALLS

Ingredients:

- 1 cup unsalted almonds, finely chopped
- 1/2 cup dried apricots, finely chopped
- 1/4 cup honey
- 1/4 cup almond flour
- 1 tsp orange zest
- 1/4 tsp ground cinnamon
- 1/4 tsp ground cardamom
- 1/8 tsp salt
- 1/4 cup unsweetened shredded coconut for coating

Instructions:

1. In a large bowl, mix together the chopped almonds, chopped apricots, honey, almond flour, orange zest, cinnamon, cardamom, and salt until well combined.
2. Use your hands to form the mixture into small balls, about the size of a walnut.
3. Roll the balls in the shredded coconut to coat them.
4. Place the balls on a baking sheet lined with parchment paper.
5. Refrigerate the balls for at least 30 minutes, or until they are firm.
6. Serve the balls chilled.

These Turkish apricot and almond balls are a delicious and healthy dessert option that's perfect for diabetic patients. The almonds provide a good source of healthy fats and protein, while the apricots are a great source of fiber and natural sweetness. The use of honey instead of sugar helps to keep the glycemic index low, while the addition of orange zest, cinnamon, and cardamom provides natural flavor without adding unnecessary sugar. The unsweetened shredded coconut provides a nice texture and flavor to the balls, while also being low in carbohydrates. This dessert is perfect for satisfying a sweet tooth without compromising on health.

CHILLED ROSEWATER PUDDING

Ingredients:

- 2 cups unsweetened almond milk
- 1/4 cup cornstarch
- 1/4 cup honey
- 2 tbsp rosewater
- 1/2 tsp ground cardamom
- 1/4 tsp vanilla extract
- 1/4 cup slivered almonds for garnish

Instructions:

1. In a small bowl, whisk together the cornstarch and 1/4 cup of almond milk until the cornstarch is fully dissolved.
2. In a medium saucepan, heat the remaining almond milk, honey, rosewater, cardamom, and vanilla extract over medium heat, stirring occasionally.
3. Once the mixture begins to simmer, add the cornstarch mixture to the saucepan and whisk continuously until the mixture thickens.
4. Remove the saucepan from the heat and let it cool for 10-15 minutes.
5. Pour the mixture into individual serving dishes or a large serving dish.
6. Refrigerate the pudding for at least 2 hours, or until it is completely chilled and set.
7. Garnish the pudding with slivered almonds before serving.

This chilled rosewater pudding is a refreshing and diabetes-friendly dessert that's perfect for hot summer days. The use of almond milk instead of cow's milk helps to keep the carbohydrate content low, while the addition of rosewater provides a unique and fragrant flavor. The use of honey instead of sugar helps to keep the glycemic index low, while the addition of cardamom and vanilla extract provides additional flavor without adding sugar. The slivered almonds provide a nice crunch and additional flavor to the pudding. Enjoy this dessert on its own or with fresh berries for an extra dose of sweetness.

TURKISH YOGURT WITH SWEET CHERRIES AND PISTACHIOS

Ingredients:

- 1 cup plain low-fat Greek yogurt
- 1/4 cup pitted sweet cherries, chopped
- 2 tbsp chopped pistachios
- 1 tbsp honey
- 1/4 tsp ground cardamom
- 1/4 tsp vanilla extract

Instructions:

1. In a small bowl, mix together the yogurt, honey, cardamom, and vanilla extract until well combined.
2. Divide the yogurt mixture into two serving dishes.
3. Top each serving with chopped sweet cherries and chopped pistachios.
4. Serve the yogurt chilled.

This Turkish yogurt with sweet cherries and pistachios is a healthy and delicious dessert option that's perfect for those with diabetes. The use of Greek yogurt provides a good source of protein and calcium, while the addition of sweet cherries provides natural sweetness and a good source of fiber. The use of honey instead of sugar helps to keep the glycemic index low, while the addition of cardamom and vanilla extract provides natural flavor without adding sugar. The chopped pistachios provide a nice crunch and additional flavor to the dish. Enjoy this dessert as a light and refreshing way to satisfy a sweet tooth.

ALMOND AND ORANGE FLOURLESS CAKE

Ingredients:

- 1 cup almond flour
- 3 large eggs, separated
- 1/2 cup honey
- 1/4 cup fresh orange juice

- 1 tbsp orange zest
- 1/4 tsp salt
- 1/4 tsp cream of tartar
- Sliced almonds for garnish

Instructions:

1. Preheat your oven to 350°F (180°C).
2. Grease a 9-inch (23 cm) round cake pan and line the bottom with parchment paper.
3. In a large mixing bowl, whisk together the almond flour, egg yolks, honey, orange juice, orange zest, and salt until well combined.
4. In a separate mixing bowl, beat the egg whites and cream of tartar together until stiff peaks form.
5. Gently fold the egg whites into the almond flour mixture until just combined.
6. Pour the batter into the prepared cake pan and sprinkle sliced almonds on top.
7. Bake for 25-30 minutes, or until the cake is lightly browned and a toothpick inserted in the center comes out clean.
8. Let the cake cool for 10-15 minutes before slicing and serving.

This almond and orange flourless cake is a gluten-free and diabetes-friendly dessert that's perfect for those with dietary restrictions. The use of almond flour instead of wheat flour helps to keep the carbohydrate content low, while the addition of honey instead of sugar helps to keep the glycemic index low. The use of fresh orange juice and zest provides a bright and citrusy flavor, while the sliced almonds on top provide a nice crunch and additional flavor to the cake. Enjoy this cake as a guilt-free dessert option that's sure to impress

PEANUT BUTTER COOKIES

Ingredients:

- 1 cup natural peanut butter (no added sugar)
- 1/2 cup almond flour
- 1/4 cup sugar substitute (e.g. erythritol)
- 1 tsp vanilla extract
- 1/4 tsp salt
- 1 large egg

Instructions:

1. Preheat the oven to 350°F (175°C) and line a baking sheet with parchment paper.
2. In a large mixing bowl, combine the peanut butter, almond flour, sugar substitute, vanilla extract, salt, and egg. Mix well to form a thick dough.
3. Use a cookie scoop or tablespoon to portion out the dough onto the prepared baking sheet, leaving about 2 inches of space between each cookie.
4. Use a fork to press down on each cookie, creating a criss-cross pattern on top.
5. Bake the cookies for 12-15 minutes, or until lightly golden around the edges.
6. Let the cookies cool on the baking sheet for 5 minutes before transferring them to a wire rack to cool completely.

COCONUT MACAROONS

Ingredients:

- 2 cups unsweetened shredded coconut
- 1/2 cup almond flour
- 1/4 cup sugar substitute (e.g. xylitol)
- 1/4 tsp salt
- 3 large egg whites
- 1 tsp vanilla extract

Instructions:

1. Preheat the oven to 350°F (175°C) and line a baking sheet with parchment paper.
2. In a large mixing bowl, combine the shredded coconut, almond flour, sugar substitute, and salt. Mix well to combine.
3. In a separate mixing bowl, whisk the egg whites and vanilla extract until stiff peaks form.
4. Gently fold the egg whites into the coconut mixture until well combined.
5. Use a cookie scoop or tablespoon to portion out the macaroons onto the prepared baking sheet, leaving about 2 inches of space between each cookie.
6. Bake the macaroons for 15-20 minutes, or until lightly golden on top.
7. Let the macaroons cool on the baking sheet.

APPLE CRISP

Ingredients:

- 4 medium-sized apples, peeled and chopped
- 1 cup almond flour
- 1/2 cup rolled oats
- 1/4 cup sugar substitute (e.g. erythritol)
- 1 tsp cinnamon
- 1/4 tsp salt
- 1/4 cup unsalted butter, melted
- 1 tsp vanilla extract

Instructions:

1. Preheat the oven to 350°F (175°C) and lightly grease a 9-inch baking dish.
2. In a large mixing bowl, combine the chopped apples, cinnamon, and sugar substitute. Mix well to coat the apples evenly.
3. Transfer the apple mixture to the prepared baking dish and spread it out evenly.
4. In a separate mixing bowl, combine the almond flour, rolled oats, salt, melted butter, and vanilla extract. Mix well to form a crumbly mixture.
5. Sprinkle the crumbly mixture over the top of the apple mixture in the baking dish.
6. Bake the apple crisp for 30-35 minutes, or until the top is golden brown and the apples are tender.
7. Let the apple crisp cool for a few minutes before serving. Optional: serve with a dollop of unsweetened whipped cream or a scoop of sugar-free ice cream.

Note: Remember to always consult with a healthcare provider or registered dietitian before making any significant changes to your diet, particularly if you have diabetes or any other health condition. They can advise you on how to incorporate these into a balanced meal plan.

LEMON CHEESECAKE BARS

Ingredients:

- 1 1/2 cups almond flour
- 1/4 cup sugar substitute (e.g. erythritol)
- 1/4 tsp salt
- 1/4 cup unsalted butter, melted
- 16 oz cream cheese, softened

- 1/2 cup plain Greek yogurt
- 1/4 cup lemon juice
- 1 tbsp lemon zest
- 2 large eggs
- Sugar substitute to taste (e.g. stevia)

Instructions:

1. Preheat the oven to 350°F (175°C) and line an 8-inch square baking dish with parchment paper.
2. In a large mixing bowl, combine the almond flour, sugar substitute, salt, and melted butter. Mix well to form a crumbly mixture.
3. Press the mixture firmly and evenly into the bottom of the prepared baking dish.
4. In a separate mixing bowl, beat the cream cheese, Greek yogurt, lemon juice, lemon zest, and sugar substitute until smooth.
5. Add the eggs to the cream cheese mixture, one at a time, mixing well after each addition.
6. Pour the cheesecake mixture over the almond flour crust in the baking dish.
7. Bake the lemon cheesecake bars for 25-30 minutes, or until the top is set and slightly golden.
8. Let the bars cool on a wire rack for 10-15 minutes before refrigerating for at least 2 hours or overnight to chill.
9. Cut the chilled cheesecake into squares and serve.

VANILLA PANNA COTTA INGREDIENTS:

- 2 cups unsweetened almond milk
- 1/4 cup sugar substitute (e.g. erythritol)
- 1 tsp vanilla extract
- 2 tsp unflavored gelatin powder
- 2 tbsp cold water

Instructions:

1. In a medium saucepan, heat the almond milk, sugar substitute, and vanilla extract over medium heat, stirring occasionally.
2. In a small bowl, sprinkle the gelatin powder over the cold water and let it sit for 5 minutes to soften.
3. Add the softened gelatin mixture to the saucepan with the almond milk mixture and stir well until the gelatin is completely dissolved.
4. Remove the saucepan from heat and let the mixture cool for a few minutes.
5. Pour the panna cotta mixture into 4 small dessert cups or ramekins.
6. Cover and refrigerate the panna cotta for at least 2 hours, or until set.
7. Serve the vanilla panna cotta chilled, topped with a few fresh berries or a sprinkle of cinnamon if desired.

STRAWBERRY CHEESECAKE BITES

Ingredients:

- 8 oz cream cheese, softened
- 1/4 cup sugar substitute (e.g. monk fruit)
- 1 tsp vanilla extract
- 1/2 cup chopped strawberries

Instructions:

1. In a large mixing bowl, beat the cream cheese until smooth and creamy.
2. Add the sugar substitute and vanilla extract to the cream cheese and beat again until well combined.
3. Fold in the chopped strawberries.
4. Use a tablespoon or small cookie scoop to portion out the cheesecake mixture into bite-sized balls.
5. Place the cheesecake bites on a parchment-lined baking sheet and freeze for 30-60 minutes, or until firm.
6. Serve the strawberry cheesecake bites chilled.

CHOCOLATE COVERED STRAWBERRIES

Ingredients:

- 12 fresh strawberries
- 1/2 cup unsweetened chocolate chips
- 1 tsp coconut oil

Instructions:

1. Line a baking sheet with parchment paper.
2. In a double boiler or microwave-safe bowl, melt the chocolate chips and coconut oil together until smooth.
3. Dip each strawberry into the melted chocolate, swirling to coat evenly.
4. Place the chocolate-covered strawberries on the prepared baking sheet and refrigerate for at least 15 minutes, or until the chocolate hardens.
5. Serve the chocolate covered strawberries chilled.

PUMPKIN SPICE
MUFFINS INGREDIENTS:

Ingredients:

- 1 1/2 cups almond flour
- 1 tsp baking powder
- 1/2 tsp baking soda
- 1/2 tsp cinnamon
- 1/2 tsp pumpkin pie spice

- 1/4 tsp salt
- 1/2 cup pumpkin puree
- 1/4 cup sugar substitute (e.g. xylitol)
- 2 large eggs
- 1 tsp vanilla extract

Instructions:

1. Preheat the oven to 350°F (175°C) and line a muffin tin with paper liners.
2. In a large mixing bowl, whisk together the almond flour, baking powder, baking soda, cinnamon, pumpkin pie spice, and salt.
3. In a separate mixing bowl, whisk together the pumpkin puree, sugar substitute, eggs, and vanilla extract until well combined.
4. Pour the wet ingredients into the dry ingredients and mix gently until a thick batter forms.
5. Use a cookie scoop or tablespoon to portion out the batter into the muffin cups, filling each one about 3/4 full. 6. Bake the muffins for 20-25 minutes, or until a toothpick inserted into the center comes out clean.
6. Let the muffins cool in the pan for a few minutes before transferring them to a wire rack to cool completely.

RASPBERRY CHIA
SEED PUDDING

Ingredients:

- 1 cup unsweetened almond milk
- 1/2 cup fresh raspberries
- 2 tbsp chia seeds
- 1/4 tsp vanilla extract
- 1 tbsp sugar substitute (e.g. stevia)

Instructions:

1. In a blender, puree the almond milk and raspberries until smooth.
2. In a mixing bowl, whisk together the raspberry puree, chia seeds, vanilla extract, and sugar substitute until well combined.
3. Let the mixture sit for 10-15 minutes to allow the chia seeds to absorb the liquid and thicken the pudding.
4. Stir the pudding again to distribute the chia seeds evenly.
5. Divide the pudding into two small jars or bowls and refrigerate for at least 1 hour, or until firm.
6. Serve the raspberry chia seed pudding chilled.

Note: These are intended as suggestions and should not replace personalized medical advice. Always consult with a healthcare provider or registered dietitian before making any significant changes to your diet, particularly if you have diabetes or any other health condition.

APRICOT AND WALNUT BALLS

Ingredients:

- 1 cup dried apricots, chopped
- 1 cup walnuts, chopped
- 1/4 cup unsweetened shredded coconut
- 1 tbsp honey
- 1/4 tsp ground cinnamon
- 1/4 tsp vanilla extract
- 1/4 cup unsweetened cocoa powder

Instructions:

1. In a large mixing bowl, mix together the chopped apricots, chopped walnuts, shredded coconut, honey, cinnamon, and vanilla extract until well combined.
2. Roll the mixture into bite-sized balls and place them on a parchment-lined baking sheet.
3. Chill the balls in the refrigerator for 30 minutes.
4. Once chilled, roll each ball in the unsweetened cocoa powder until coated.
5. Serve the apricot and walnut balls chilled.

These apricot and walnut balls are a simple and healthy dessert option that's perfect for those with diabetes. The use of dried apricots provides natural sweetness and a good source of fiber, while the walnuts provide a good source of healthy fats and protein. The use of honey instead of sugar helps to keep the glycemic index low, while the addition of cinnamon and vanilla extract provides natural flavor without adding sugar. The unsweetened shredded coconut and unsweetened cocoa powder provide a nice texture and additional flavor to the balls. Enjoy these apricot and walnut balls as a guilt-free dessert option that's perfect for satisfying a sweet tooth.

PUMPKIN PUDDING

Ingredients:

- 1 cup pumpkin puree
- 1/2 cup unsweetened almond milk
- 2 tbsp cornstarch
- 1/4 cup honey
- 1 tsp ground cinnamon
- 1/4 tsp ground ginger
- 1/4 tsp ground nutmeg
- 1/4 tsp salt
- 1/2 cup unsweetened whipped cream (optional)

Instructions:

1. In a medium saucepan, whisk together the pumpkin puree, almond milk, cornstarch, honey, cinnamon, ginger, nutmeg, and salt until well combined.
2. Place the saucepan over medium heat and cook the mixture, stirring constantly, for 5-7 minutes, or until it thickens and starts to boil.
3. Reduce the heat to low and let the mixture simmer for an additional 2-3 minutes, stirring occasionally.
4. Remove the saucepan from the heat and let the mixture cool to room temperature.
5. Once cooled, divide the mixture evenly among 4 dessert bowls or ramekins.
6. Cover the bowls with plastic wrap and refrigerate for at least 2 hours, or until set.
7. Serve the pumpkin pudding chilled, topped with a dollop of unsweetened whipped cream, if desired.

This pumpkin pudding is a delicious and healthy dessert option that's perfect for those with diabetes. The use of pumpkin provides a good source of fiber and vitamins, while the addition of honey instead of sugar helps to keep the glycemic index low. The use of almond milk instead of dairy milk provides a good source of calcium and healthy fats, while the warming spices like cinnamon, ginger, and nutmeg provide a warm and comforting flavor. Enjoy this pumpkin pudding as a guilt-free dessert option that's perfect for fall.

PEANUT BUTTER CHOCOLATE CHIP COOKIES

Ingredients:

- 1 cup creamy peanut butter
- 1/2 cup sugar substitute (e.g. erythritol)
- 2 large eggs
- 1 tsp vanilla extract
- 1/2 tsp baking powder
- 1/2 tsp salt
- 1/2 cup sugar-free chocolate chips

Instructions:

1. Preheat the oven to 350°F (175°C) and line a baking sheet with parchment paper.
2. In a large mixing bowl, beat the peanut butter and sugar substitute until well combined.
3. Add the eggs, vanilla extract, baking powder, and salt to the peanut butter mixture and beat again until smooth.
4. Fold in the sugar-free chocolate chips.
5. Use a cookie scoop or tablespoon to portion out the cookie dough onto the prepared baking sheet.
6. Bake the cookies for 12-15 minutes, or until the edges are lightly golden.
7. Let the cookies cool on the baking sheet for a few minutes before transferring them to a wire rack to cool completely.

BLUEBERRY LEMON BARS

Ingredients:

- 1 cup almond flour
- 1/4 cup coconut flour
- 1/4 cup sugar substitute (e.g. monk fruit)
- 1/2 tsp baking powder
- 1/4 tsp salt

- 1/2 cup unsalted butter, melted
- 2 large eggs
- 1/4 cup lemon juice
- 1 tbsp lemon zest
- 1/2 cup fresh blueberries

Instructions:

1. Preheat the oven to 350°F (175°C) and line an 8x8-inch baking pan with parchment paper.
2. In a large mixing bowl, whisk together the almond flour, coconut flour, sugar substitute, baking powder, and salt.
3. Add the melted butter, eggs, lemon juice, and lemon zest to the dry ingredients and whisk again until well combined.
4. Fold in the fresh blueberries.
5. Pour the batter into the prepared baking pan and smooth out the top.
6. Bake the bars for 20-25 minutes, or until lightly golden and set.
7. Let the bars cool in the pan for a few minutes before transferring them to a wire rack to cool completely.

DATE AND WALNUT COOKIES

Ingredients:

- 1 cup almond flour
- 1/2 cup chopped walnuts
- 1/2 cup chopped dates
- 1 tsp baking powder

- 1/4 tsp salt
- 1 large egg
- 1 tbsp honey
- 1 tsp vanilla extract

Instructions:

1. Preheat your oven to 350°F (175°C). Line a baking sheet with parchment paper.
2. In a large mixing bowl, whisk together the almond flour, chopped walnuts, chopped dates, baking powder, and salt until well combined.
3. Add the egg, honey, and vanilla extract to the mixing bowl and stir until the batter is smooth.
4. Drop spoonful of the batter onto the prepared baking sheet, spacing them about 1 inch apart.
5. Bake the cookies for 12-15 minutes, or until they're lightly golden brown.
6. Remove the cookies from the oven and let them cool on the baking sheet for 5 minutes before transferring them to a wire rack to cool completely.

These date and walnut cookies are a healthy and delicious dessert option that's perfect for those with diabetes. The use of almond flour instead of wheat flour helps to keep the glycemic index low, while the addition of chopped walnuts and dates provides a good source of healthy fats and fiber. The use of honey instead of sugar provides a natural sweetener that won't spike blood sugar levels. Enjoy these cookies as a guilt-free dessert option that's perfect for satisfying your sweet tooth.

YOGURT AND FRUIT PARFAIT

Ingredients:

- 1 cup plain Greek yogurt
- 1/4 cup chopped strawberries
- 1/4 cup chopped kiwi
- 1/4 cup blueberries
- 1 tbsp honey
- 1/4 cup chopped almonds

Instructions:

1. In a small mixing bowl, combine the Greek yogurt and honey until well mixed.
2. In a separate bowl, mix the chopped strawberries, kiwi, and blueberries.
3. In a glass, spoon a layer of the yogurt mixture, followed by a layer of the mixed fruit, and then a layer of chopped almonds.
4. Repeat the layering until the glass is full, ending with a layer of chopped almonds on top.
5. Refrigerate the parfait for at least 30 minutes before serving.

This yogurt and fruit parfait is a healthy and refreshing dessert option that's perfect for those with diabetes. The use of Greek yogurt instead of regular yogurt helps to keep the glycemic index low, while the addition of fresh fruit provides a good source of vitamins and antioxidants. The use of honey instead of sugar provides a natural sweetener that won't spike blood sugar levels

TURKISH SEMOLINA HALVA
WITH PISTACHIOS

Ingredients:

- 1 cup fine semolina
- 1 cup water
- 1 cup milk (low-fat or skim milk can be used)
- 1/2 cup unsalted butter

- 1/2 cup sweetener (such as stevia, erythritol, or Splenda)
- 1/2 cup shelled pistachios, roughly chopped

Instructions:

1. In a medium-sized pot, melt the butter over medium heat. Add the semolina and stir constantly for 7-8 minutes until it turns golden brown.
2. In a separate pot, heat the water and milk until it comes to a boil.
3. Gradually pour the hot milk and water mixture into the semolina mixture while stirring constantly. Be careful, as it may splatter.
4. Reduce heat to low and continue stirring for 5 minutes until the mixture thickens.
5. Add the sweetener and continue stirring for another 5 minutes until it reaches the desired consistency.
6. Remove from heat and let it cool for a few minutes before transferring to a serving dish.
7. Sprinkle the chopped pistachios over the halva and serve warm or chilled.

This Turkish semolina halva is a perfect dessert option for diabetic patients as it contains healthy fats, fiber, and protein from the pistachios and low glycemic index carbohydrates from semolina. The use of low-calorie sweeteners instead of sugar also makes it a diabetes-friendly option. Enjoy!

MANGO LASSI
(MANGO YOGURT SMOOTHIE)

Ingredients:

- 1 ripe mango, peeled and chopped
- 1 cup plain low-fat yogurt
- 1/2 cup unsweetened almond milk
- 1/2 teaspoon cardamom powder
- 1 tablespoon honey (optional)
- 1/4 cup crushed ice
- Sliced almonds for garnish

Instructions:

1. In a blender, combine the chopped mango, yogurt, almond milk, cardamom powder, and honey (if using).
2. Blend the ingredients until smooth and creamy.
3. Add the crushed ice and blend again until smooth.
4. Pour the mixture into glasses and garnish with sliced almonds.
5. Serve immediately and enjoy!

This Mango Lassi is a refreshing and healthy dessert option for diabetic patients. The use of low-fat yogurt and almond milk makes it low in sugar and high in protein and healthy fats. The addition of cardamom powder provides a unique and aromatic flavor to this classic Pakistani smoothie. Enjoy this delicious and satisfying dessert.

DATE AND PISTACHIO TRUFFLES

Ingredients:

- 1 cup pitted dates
- 1/2 cup unsalted pistachios, chopped
- 2 tablespoons cocoa powder
- 1/4 teaspoon ground cinnamon
- 1/4 teaspoon ground cardamom
- 1/4 teaspoon sea salt
- 1/2 teaspoon vanilla extract
- 2 tablespoons unsweetened shredded coconut, for rolling

Directions:

1. In a food processor, pulse the dates until they form a smooth paste.
2. Add the chopped pistachios, cocoa powder, cinnamon, cardamom, sea salt, and vanilla extract to the food processor. Pulse until all the ingredients are well combined.
3. Roll the mixture into small, bite-sized balls.
4. Spread the shredded coconut onto a plate. Roll each truffle in the coconut until well coated.
5. Place the truffles on a baking sheet and refrigerate for at least 30 minutes before serving.

These date and pistachio truffles are a delicious, diabetes-friendly dessert option that draws inspiration from the flavors of the Middle East. The dates provide natural sweetness, while the pistachios add a satisfying crunch. The cocoa powder and spices create a rich, complex flavor profile, while the shredded coconut adds a touch of tropical flair. This is easy to make and can be customized to suit individual tastes. Best of all, it's a dessert that can be enjoyed by everyone, regardless of their dietary restrictions.

BAKED RICOTTA WITH BERRIES

Ingredients:

- 1 cup part-skim ricotta cheese
- 1/4 cup honey
- 1 egg
- 1 teaspoon vanilla extract
- 1/4 teaspoon ground cinnamon
- 1/4 cup fresh berries (such as strawberries, raspberries, or blueberries)

Directions:

1. Preheat the oven to 350°F (175°C).
2. In a mixing bowl, combine the ricotta cheese, honey, egg, vanilla extract, and cinnamon. Mix well.
3. Pour the mixture into a small baking dish.
4. Bake for 25-30 minutes, or until the top is lightly golden and the center is set.
5. Remove from the oven and let cool for 10 minutes.
6. Top with fresh berries and serve.

This baked ricotta dessert is a delicious and satisfying option that's inspired by Italian cuisine. The ricotta cheese provides a creamy, protein-rich base, while the honey adds natural sweetness. The egg helps to bind everything together, and the vanilla extract and cinnamon add warm, comforting flavors. Topping the baked ricotta with fresh berries adds a burst of fresh, fruity flavor and additional antioxidants. This dessert is easy to make and can be enjoyed as a snack or as a sweet ending to any meal.

GREEK YOGURT PARFAIT
WITH NUTS AND BERRIES

Ingredients:

- 1 cup plain Greek yogurt
- 1/4 cup chopped mixed nuts (such as almonds, pecans, and walnuts)
- 1/4 cup fresh berries (such as blueberries, raspberries, or strawberries)
- 1 tablespoon honey (optional)

Directions:

1. In a small bowl, mix together the Greek yogurt and honey (if using).
2. Layer the yogurt mixture, chopped nuts, and fresh berries in a serving glass.
3. Repeat the layering process until you reach the top of the glass.
4. Serve immediately or refrigerate until ready to serve.

This Greek yogurt parfait with nuts and berries is a refreshing and diabetes-friendly dessert option that's inspired by the Mediterranean diet. The Greek yogurt is high in protein and low in sugar, while the nuts provide healthy fats and fiber. The fresh berries add natural sweetness and a boost of antioxidants. This dessert is simple to make and can be customized with your favorite nuts and berries. It's perfect for a quick and easy snack or a light, healthy dessert after a meal.

VANILLA AND ALMOND MILK CUSTARD

Ingredients:

- 2 cups unsweetened almond milk
- 2 tablespoons cornstarch
- 2 egg yolks
- 1/4 cup honey or maple syrup
- 1 teaspoon vanilla extract
- 1/4 teaspoon ground cinnamon
- 1/4 teaspoon ground nutmeg

Directions:

1. In a small bowl, whisk together the almond milk and cornstarch until well combined.
2. In a separate mixing bowl, whisk together the egg yolks, honey or maple syrup, vanilla extract, cinnamon, and nutmeg.
3. Slowly pour the almond milk mixture into the egg yolk mixture, whisking constantly to combine.
4. Pour the mixture into a small saucepan and cook over medium heat, stirring constantly, for 5-7 minutes or until the custard thickens and coats the back of a spoon.
5. Remove from heat and let cool for a few minutes.
6. Divide the custard into individual serving dishes and chill in the refrigerator for at least 1 hour before serving.

This vanilla and almond milk custard is a delicious and diabetes-friendly dessert option that's perfect for those who are looking to manage their blood sugar levels. The almond milk provides a low-carb, low-sugar alternative to regular milk, while the honey or maple syrup adds natural sweetness. The vanilla extract and spices create a warm, comforting flavor profile that's perfect for any time of year. This custard is easy to make and can be enjoyed as a simple dessert or as a light, healthy snack

COCONUT LADOO

Ingredients:

- 1 cup unsweetened shredded coconut
- 1/4 cup coconut flour
- 1/4 cup honey or maple syrup
- 1/4 cup coconut oil
- 1 teaspoon ground cardamom
- 1/4 teaspoon ground cinnamon
- 1/4 teaspoon ground nutmeg
- 1/4 teaspoon salt

Directions:

1. In a mixing bowl, combine the shredded coconut, coconut flour, cardamom, cinnamon, nutmeg, and salt. Mix well.
2. In a small saucepan, heat the honey or maple syrup and coconut oil over low heat, stirring constantly, until the mixture is smooth and well combined.
3. Pour the honey and coconut oil mixture into the mixing bowl with the coconut mixture. Mix well.
4. Using a cookie scoop or tablespoon, form the mixture into small balls and place them on a lined baking sheet.
5. Refrigerate the balls for 15-20 minutes, or until they are firm.
6. Store the coconut ladoo in an airtight container in the refrigerator until ready to serve.

This coconut ladoo is a diabetes-friendly dessert that's inspired by Indian cuisine. The shredded coconut and coconut flour provide a low-carb, low-sugar base, while the honey or maple syrup adds natural sweetness. The coconut oil provides healthy fats and helps to bind everything together. The spices, including cardamom, cinnamon, and nutmeg, add a warm, aromatic flavor that's reminiscent of traditional Indian sweets. This dessert is easy to make and can be enjoyed as a healthy snack or a sweet ending to any meal.

PECAN PIE BARS

Ingredients:

- 2 cups almond flour
- 1/2 cup coconut flour
- 1/4 tsp salt
- 1/4 cup unsweetened applesauce
- 1/4 cup coconut oil, melted
- 1/4 cup low-calorie sweetener (such as erythritol)
- 2 eggs
- 2 tsp vanilla extract
- 1 1/2 cups chopped pecans
- 1/4 cup sugar-free maple syrup

Instructions:

1. Preheat the oven to 350°F and line an 8x8-inch baking dish with parchment paper.
2. In a large mixing bowl, whisk together the almond flour, coconut flour, and salt.
3. Add in the applesauce, melted coconut oil, and low-calorie sweetener, and mix until well combined.
4. Beat in the eggs and vanilla extract until the mixture is smooth.
5. Fold in the chopped pecans, reserving a few for topping.
6. Pour the mixture into the prepared baking dish, smoothing it out into an even layer.
7. Drizzle the sugar-free maple syrup over the top of the mixture and sprinkle the reserved pecans on top.
8. Bake for 25-30 minutes, or until the bars are golden brown and set.
9. Allow to cool completely in the pan, then cut into bars and serve.

These Pecan Pie Bars for Diabetics are a perfect dessert option for those with diabetes who still want to enjoy the flavors of the South. They are made with low-glycemic index ingredients like almond flour and coconut flour, and sweetened with a sugar-free maple syrup. The addition of pecans provides a delicious crunch and nutty flavor that will leave you wanting more. Enjoy!

RICOTTA CHEESECAKE
WITH BERRY COMPOTE

Ingredients:

- 1 1/2 cups almond flour
- 1/4 cup low-calorie sweetener (such as erythritol)
- 1/4 cup coconut oil, melted
- 2 cups part-skim ricotta cheese
- 1/4 cup low-fat cream cheese
- 2 eggs
- 2 tsp vanilla extract
- 1/4 tsp salt
- 1 cup mixed berries (such as raspberries, blueberries, and strawberries)
- 1 tbsp low-calorie sweetener
- 1 tbsp water

Instructions:

1. Preheat the oven to 350°F and lightly grease a 9-inch pie dish with coconut oil.
2. In a mixing bowl, combine the almond flour, low-calorie sweetener, and melted coconut oil until it forms a crumbly mixture.
3. Press the mixture into the bottom of the prepared pie dish to form an even crust.
4. In another mixing bowl, whisk together the ricotta cheese, cream cheese, eggs, vanilla extract, and salt until smooth and well combined.
5. Pour the mixture into the prepared crust and smooth out the surface.
6. Bake for 35-40 minutes or until the cheesecake is set and golden brown.
7. While the cheesecake is baking, prepare the berry compote by combining the mixed berries, low-calorie sweetener, and water in a small saucepan over medium heat.
8. Bring the mixture to a simmer and cook for 5-7 minutes, stirring occasionally, until the berries have softened and the mixture has thickened.
9. Once the cheesecake is baked, remove it from the oven and let it cool to room temperature.
10. Serve the cheesecake slices with the warm berry compote on top.

This Ricotta Cheesecake with Berry Compote is a diabetes-friendly dessert option that is inspired by the flavors of Italy. It is made with almond flour instead of regular flour, which makes it low in carbohydrates, and sweetened with a low-calorie sweetener. The berry compote adds a tangy and sweet flavor to the creamy cheesecake that will leave you feeling satisfied. Enjoy this Italian-inspired dessert with your friends and family!

CHURRO BITES WITH SPICED CHOCOLATE SAUCE

Ingredients:

For the churro bites:

- 1/2 cup almond flour
- 1/4 cup coconut flour
- 1/4 cup low-calorie sweetener (such as erythritol)
- 1 tsp baking powder
- 1 tsp ground cinnamon
- 1/4 cup coconut oil, melted
- 2 eggs
- 1 tsp vanilla extract

For the spiced chocolate sauce:

- 1/2 cup unsweetened almond milk
- 1/4 cup dark chocolate chips
- 1/4 tsp ground cinnamon
- 1/4 tsp ground cayenne pepper

Instructions:

1. Preheat the oven to 350°F and line a baking sheet with parchment paper.
2. In a mixing bowl, whisk together the almond flour, coconut flour, low-calorie sweetener, baking powder, and ground cinnamon.
3. In another mixing bowl, whisk together the melted coconut oil, eggs, and vanilla extract.
4. Add the wet ingredients to the dry ingredients and mix until a thick batter forms.
5. Scoop out a tablespoon of batter and roll into small balls using your hands.
6. Place the balls on the prepared baking sheet and bake for 15-18 minutes or until golden brown.
7. While the churro bites are baking, prepare the spiced chocolate sauce by heating the almond milk in a small saucepan over medium heat.
8. Once the milk starts to simmer, remove from heat and add the dark chocolate chips, cinnamon, and cayenne pepper.

9. Whisk the mixture until the chocolate is melted and the sauce is smooth.

10. Serve the churro bites with the spiced chocolate sauce on the side for dipping.

These Churro Bites with Spiced Chocolate Sauce are a diabetes-friendly dessert option that is inspired by the flavors of Mexico. Instead of using regular flour, it uses almond and coconut flour which makes them lower in carbs. The spiced chocolate sauce is a unique twist on a classic dessert dip, with a hint of cinnamon and cayenne pepper adding a subtle kick. Enjoy these delicious bites with a cup of hot tea or coffee!

CHOCOLATE PEANUT BUTTER CUPS

Ingredients:

- 1/2 cup sugar-free chocolate chips
- 1/4 cup natural peanut butter
- 1/4 cup coconut oil
- 1/4 cup sugar substitute (e.g. erythritol)

Instructions:

1. Line a muffin tin with 6 paper liners.
2. In a microwave-safe bowl, melt the chocolate chips and coconut oil in 30-second increments until fully melted and combined.
3. Spoon 1 tablespoon of the chocolate mixture into each of the paper liners.
4. In a separate mixing bowl, stir together the peanut butter and sugar substitute until well combined.
5. Spoon 1 tablespoon of the peanut butter mixture on top of the chocolate in each of the paper liners.
6. Top the peanut butter mixture with the remaining chocolate mixture, dividing it evenly among the cups.
7. Refrigerate the chocolate peanut butter cups for at least 30 minutes, or until firm.
8. Peel off the paper liners and serve the chocolate peanut butter cups chilled.

CINNAMON APPLESAUCE CAKE

Ingredients:

- 2 cups almond flour
- 1/2 cup sugar substitute (e.g. monk fruit)
- 1 tsp baking powder
- 1 tsp ground cinnamon
- 1/4 tsp salt
- 1 cup unsweetened applesauce
- 2 large eggs
- 1/4 cup unsalted butter, melted
- 1 tsp vanilla extract

Instructions:

1. Preheat the oven to 350°F (175°C) and grease an 8-inch square baking pan.
2. In a large mixing bowl, whisk together the almond flour, sugar substitute, baking powder, cinnamon, and salt.
3. In a separate mixing bowl, whisk together the applesauce, eggs, melted butter, and vanilla extract.
4. Add the wet ingredients to the dry ingredients and stir until a smooth batter forms.
5. Pour the batter into the prepared baking pan and smooth the top with a spatula.
6. Bake the cake for 25-30 minutes, or until a toothpick inserted into the center comes out clean.
7. Let the cake cool in the pan for a few minutes before transferring it to a wire rack to cool completely.

NO-BAKE PEANUT BUTTER BALLS

Ingredients:

- 1 cup creamy peanut butter
- 1/4 cup honey
- 1/4 cup chopped nuts (such as almonds or walnuts)
- 1/4 cup unsweetened shredded coconut
- 1/4 cup ground flaxseed
- Pinch of salt

Instructions:

1. In a bowl, mix together the peanut butter, honey, chopped nuts, shredded coconut, ground flaxseed, and salt.
2. Roll the mixture into small balls and place them on a baking sheet lined with parchment paper.
3. Chill the peanut butter balls in the refrigerator for at least 30 minutes before serving.

Enjoy the non-baked balls!

SUGAR-FREE CHEESECAKE

Ingredients:

For the crust:

- 1 cup almond flour
- 1/4 cup melted butter

- 1/4 cup granulated sugar substitute
- 1 tsp cinnamon

For the filling:

- 16 oz cream cheese, softened
- 1/2 cup granulated sugar substitute

- 2 tsp vanilla extract
- 2 eggs

Instructions:

1. Preheat the oven to 350°F (180°C).
2. In a bowl, mix together the almond flour, melted butter, sugar substitute, and cinnamon.
3. Press the crust mixture into the bottom of a 9-inch spring form pan.
4. In a separate bowl, beat the cream cheese, sugar substitute, and vanilla extract until smooth.
5. Beat in the eggs, one at a time, until well combined.
6. Pour the filling over the crust and smooth out the top.
7. Bake for 35-40 minutes, or until the cheesecake is set and the edges are golden brown.
8. Chill the cheesecake in the refrigerator for at least 2 hours before serving.

SUGAR-FREE BANANA BREAD

Ingredients:

- 1 cup almond flour
- 1/4 cup coconut flour
- 1 tsp baking powder
- 1/2 tsp baking soda
- 1/4 tsp salt

- 3 ripe bananas, mashed
- 3 eggs
- 1/4 cup melted coconut oil
- 1 tsp vanilla extract
- 1/4 cup granulated sugar substitute

Instructions:

1. Preheat the oven to 350°F (180°C).
2. In a bowl, mix together the almond flour, coconut flour, baking powder, baking soda, and salt.
3. In a separate bowl, whisk together the mashed bananas, eggs, melted coconut oil, vanilla extract, and sugar substitute.
4. Add the dry ingredients to the wet ingredients and stir until well combined.
5. Pour the batter into a greased loaf pan.
6. Bake for 50-60 minutes, or until a toothpick inserted into the center of the bread comes out clean.
7. Cut the bread and enjoy with tea.

SUGAR-FREE BLUEBERRY LEMON BARS

Ingredients:

For the crust:

- 1 cup almond flour
- 1/4 cup melted butter
- 1/4 cup granulated sugar substitute
- 1/4 tsp salt

For the filling:

- 2 cups fresh blueberries
- 1/4 cup lemon juice
- 1/4 cup granulated sugar substitute
- 1/4 cup cornstarch

Instructions:

1. Preheat the oven to 350°F (180°C).
2. In a bowl, mix together the almond flour, melted butter, sugar substitute, and salt.
3. Press the crust mixture into the bottom of a 9-inch square baking dish.
4. In a separate bowl, mix together the blueberries, lemon juice, sugar substitute, and cornstarch.
5. Pour the blueberry mixture over the crust and spread it out evenly.
6. Bake for 30-35 minutes, or until the filling is set and the edges are golden brown.
7. Let the bars cool in the baking dish for a few minutes before cutting them into squares.

Enjoy!

SUGAR-FREE CHOCOLATE MOUSSE

Ingredients:

- 1 cup heavy cream
- 1/2 cup unsweetened cocoa powder
- 1/4 cup granulated sweetener (such as erythritol or stevia)
- 1 teaspoon vanilla extract
- 1/4 teaspoon salt
- Optional toppings: whipped cream, chopped nuts, grated chocolate

Instructions:

1. In a large mixing bowl, add heavy cream, cocoa powder, sweetener, vanilla extract, and salt.
2. Using an electric mixer beat the mixture until it becomes thick and creamy. This should take about 3-5 minutes on medium speed.
3. Once the mixture has thickened, spoon it into small serving cups or ramekins.
4. Chill the chocolate mousse in the refrigerator for at least 2 hours or until set.
5. Before serving, top with whipped cream, chopped nuts, or grated chocolate, if desired.

Enjoy your delicious, sugar-free chocolate mousse dessert! This is perfect for people with diabetes or anyone who wants to enjoy a guilt-free dessert.

PISTACHIO HALVA

Ingredients:

- 1 cup unsalted pistachios
- 1/2 cup unsweetened tahini
- 1/4 cup granulated sweetener (such as erythritol or stevia)
- 1/4 cup water
- 1/4 teaspoon ground cardamom

Instructions:

1. Preheat the oven to 350°F (180°C).
2. Spread the pistachios evenly on a baking sheet and roast for 5-7 minutes or until lightly toasted.
3. In a saucepan, combine tahini, sweetener, and water.
4. Cook over medium heat, stirring constantly, until the mixture thickens and becomes smooth.
5. Add the toasted pistachios and cardamom to the tahini mixture.
6. Stir until the ingredients are evenly distributed and the mixture is smooth.
7. Pour the mixture into a square baking dish and smooth the surface with a spatula.
8. Refrigerate the mixture for at least 1 hour or until firm.
9. Cut the halva into small squares and serve.

Enjoy your delicious and healthy pistachio halva, a traditional dessert from the Middle East that is suitable for people with diabetes! This uses natural sweeteners from tahini and is packed with healthy fats and protein from pistachios, making it a great dessert option for anyone looking for a satisfying and healthy treat.

SWISS APPLE CRUMBLE

Ingredients:

- 3 cups thinly sliced apples (about 3 medium apples)
- 1/2 cup almond flour
- 1/2 cup old-fashioned rolled oats
- 1/4 cup granulated sweetener (such as erythritol or stevia)
- 1/4 cup unsalted butter, melted
- 1 teaspoon ground cinnamon
- Pinch of salt

Instructions:

1. Preheat the oven to 375°F (190°C).
2. In a mixing bowl, combine sliced apples, almond flour, oats, sweetener, melted butter, cinnamon, and salt.
3. Mix the ingredients until the apple slices are coated with the mixture.
4. Transfer the mixture to a baking dish.
5. Bake the apple crumble for 30-35 minutes or until the top is golden brown and the apples are tender.
6. Serve the apple crumble warm or at room temperature.

Enjoy your delicious and healthy Swiss apple crumble! This is a twist on a classic dessert and is packed with fiber and healthy fats from almond flour and oats. It also uses natural sweeteners, making it a great dessert option for people with diabetes.

GREEK YOGURT FRUIT TART

Ingredients:

- 1 cup almond flour
- 1/4 cup coconut oil, melted
- 2 tablespoons granulated sweetener (such as erythritol or stevia)
- 1 teaspoon vanilla extract

- 1 cup plain Greek yogurt
- 1/4 cup honey
- 1 teaspoon vanilla extract
- Assorted fresh fruit (such as berries, kiwi, and mango), sliced

Instructions:

1. Preheat the oven to 350°F (180°C).
2. In a mixing bowl, combine almond flour, melted coconut oil, sweetener, and vanilla extract.
3. Mix the ingredients until a dough forms.
4. Press the dough into a 9-inch tart pan, making sure to press it evenly across the bottom and up the sides.
5. Bake the crust for 10-12 minutes or until golden brown.
6. In a separate mixing bowl, combine Greek yogurt, honey, and vanilla extract.
7. Mix the ingredients until the mixture is smooth and creamy.
8. Spread the yogurt mixture evenly over the cooled crust.
9. Top the tart with sliced fresh fruit, arranging the fruit in a decorative pattern.
10. Chill the tart in the refrigerator for at least 1 hour or until the yogurt mixture is set.

Enjoy your delicious and healthy Greek yogurt fruit tart! This is packed with protein and healthy fats from almond flour and Greek yogurt, and uses natural sweeteners from honey and fresh fruit. It is a refreshing and satisfying dessert option that is sure to be enjoyed by all.

ALMOND BUTTER COOKIES

Ingredients:

- 1/2 cup almond flour
- 1/2 cup unsweetened almond butter
- 1/4 cup granulated sweetener (such as erythritol or stevia)
- 1 egg
- 1/2 teaspoon baking powder
- 1/4 teaspoon salt
- 1/2 teaspoon vanilla extract

Instructions:

1. Preheat the oven to 350°F (180°C).
2. In a mixing bowl, combine almond flour, almond butter, sweetener, egg, baking powder, salt, and vanilla extract.
3. Mix the ingredients until well combined and a dough forms.
4. Scoop the dough by rounded tablespoons onto a baking sheet lined with parchment paper.
5. Flatten the cookies with a fork or the bottom of a glass.
6. Bake the cookies for 10-12 minutes or until golden brown.
7. Allow the cookies to cool on the baking sheet for 5 minutes, then transfer them to a wire rack to cool completely.

Enjoy your delicious and healthy almond butter cookies! This is packed with healthy fats from almond flour and almond butter and uses natural sweeteners. The cookies are low in carbohydrates, making them a great option for people with diabetes. These cookies are a satisfying and easy-to-make dessert that can be enjoyed anytime.

BESAN LADOO

Ingredients:

- 2 cups besan flour (chickpea flour)
- 1/2 cup unsalted butter or ghee, melted
- 1/2 cup granulated sweetener (such as erythritol or stevia)
- 1/4 cup chopped almonds or cashews
- 1/2 teaspoon ground cardamom

Instructions:

1. Heat a non-stick pan over medium heat.
2. Add the besan flour to the pan and roast it for 10-12 minutes or until the flour becomes fragrant and changes color slightly.
3. Remove the pan from heat and let the besan flour cool to room temperature.
4. In a mixing bowl, combine the cooled besan flour, melted butter or ghee, sweetener, chopped nuts, and ground cardamom.
5. Mix the ingredients until well combined and a dough forms.
6. Using your hands, roll the dough into small balls (ladoos).
7. Place the ladoos on a plate or tray lined with parchment paper and let them set for 30 minutes.
8. Serve and enjoy your delicious and healthy besan ladoos!

This is packed with protein and fiber from the chickpea flour and nuts, and uses natural sweeteners. The ladoos are low in carbohydrates, making them a great option for people with diabetes. This is a traditional Indian dessert that is easy to make and can be enjoyed as a guilt-free treat.

PEANUT BUTTER BANANA OATMEAL COOKIES

Ingredients:

- 1 cup quick-cooking oats
- 1/2 cup creamy peanut butter
- 1 ripe banana, mashed
- 1/4 cup unsweetened applesauce
- 1/4 cup granulated sweetener (such as erythritol or stevia)
- 1 teaspoon baking powder
- 1/4 teaspoon salt
- 1/4 cup chopped peanuts (optional)

Instructions:

1. Preheat the oven to 350°F (180°C).
2. In a mixing bowl, combine oats, peanut butter, mashed banana, applesauce, sweetener, baking powder, and salt.
3. Mix the ingredients until well combined and a dough forms.
4. If desired, fold in chopped peanuts into the dough.
5. Scoop the dough into 12-14 portions and place them on a baking sheet lined with parchment paper.
6. Flatten the dough balls slightly with your hand.
7. Bake the cookies for 12-15 minutes or until the edges are lightly golden.
8. Allow the cookies to cool on the baking sheet for 5 minutes, then transfer them to a wire rack to cool completely.

Enjoy your delicious and healthy peanut butter banana oatmeal cookies! This is packed with fiber and healthy fats from oats and peanuts, and uses natural sweeteners. The cookies are low in carbohydrates, making them a great option for people with diabetes. The combination of peanut butter and banana provides a sweet and nutty flavor that is sure to satisfy your sweet tooth. These cookies make for a great snack or dessert option.

MAPLE WALNUT COOKIES

Ingredients:

- 1 cup almond flour
- 1/4 cup chopped walnuts
- 1/4 cup granulated sweetener (such as erythritol or stevia)
- 1/4 cup unsalted butter, softened
- 1 tablespoon pure maple syrup
- 1/2 teaspoon vanilla extract
- 1/4 teaspoon baking powder
- Pinch of salt

Instructions:

1. Preheat the oven to 350°F (180°C).
2. In a mixing bowl, combine almond flour, chopped walnuts, sweetener, softened butter, maple syrup, vanilla extract, baking powder, and salt.
3. Mix the ingredients until well combined and a dough forms.
4. Scoop the dough into 12-14 portions and place them on a baking sheet lined with parchment paper.
5. Flatten the dough balls slightly with your hand.
6. Bake the cookies for 12-15 minutes or until the edges are lightly golden.
7. Allow the cookies to cool on the baking sheet for 5 minutes, then transfer them to a wire rack to cool completely.

Enjoy your delicious and healthy maple walnut cookies! This is packed with healthy fats from almond flour and walnuts, and uses natural sweeteners. The cookies are low in carbohydrates, making them a great option for people with diabetes. The use of pure maple syrup gives the cookies a distinct Canadian flavor, and the combination of maple and walnut provides a sweet and nutty taste. These cookies make for a great snack or dessert option.

LAVENDER HONEY CHEESECAKE

Ingredients:

For the crust:

- 1 cup almond flour
- 1/4 cup granulated sweetener (such as erythritol or stevia)
- 1/4 cup unsalted butter, melted

For the filling:

- 16 oz cream cheese, softened
- 1/2 cup granulated sweetener (such as erythritol or stevia)
- 2 tablespoons fresh lavender flowers
- 2 tablespoons honey
- 1/2 teaspoon vanilla extract
- 2 large eggs
- 1/4 cup heavy cream

Instructions:

1. Preheat the oven to 325°F (160°C).
2. In a mixing bowl, combine almond flour, sweetener, and melted butter for the crust.
3. Mix the ingredients until well combined and a dough forms.
4. Press the dough into the bottom of a 9-inch springform pan.
5. Bake the crust for 10 minutes, then remove from the oven and set aside to cool.
6. In a mixing bowl, beat cream cheese until smooth.
7. Add sweetener, fresh lavender flowers, honey, and vanilla extract, and beat until well combined.
8. Add eggs one at a time, beating well after each addition.
9. Stir in heavy cream and mix until smooth.
10. Pour the filling onto the cooled crust.
11. Bake for 40-45 minutes, or until the center is set.
12. Allow the cheesecake to cool at room temperature for 30 minutes, then refrigerate for at least 2 hours before serving.

Enjoy your delicious and unique lavender honey cheesecake! This combines the floral taste of lavender with the sweetness of honey and cream cheese, creating a decadent and fragrant dessert that is perfect for any occasion. The almond flour crust is a low-carb alternative to traditional graham cracker crusts, making it ideal for people with diabetes.

CARDAMOM PISTACHIO PUDDING

Ingredients:

- 2 cups unsweetened almond milk
- 1/4 cup granulated sweetener (such as erythritol or stevia)
- 1/4 cup cornstarch
- 1/4 teaspoon ground cardamom
- 1/4 teaspoon vanilla extract
- 1/4 cup unsalted pistachios, finely chopped

Instructions:

1. In a medium saucepan, whisk together almond milk, sweetener, cornstarch, and cardamom until well combined.
2. Heat the mixture over medium heat, whisking constantly, until it thickens and comes to a boil.
3. Reduce heat to low and simmer for 2-3 minutes, continuing to whisk until the mixture becomes very thick.
4. Remove from heat and stir in vanilla extract.
5. Pour the pudding into four small bowls or ramekins and let them cool for a few minutes.
6. Sprinkle finely chopped pistachios over the top of each pudding.
7. Refrigerate the puddings for at least 2 hours or until chilled and set.

Enjoy your delicious and unique cardamom pistachio pudding! This features the traditional Middle Eastern flavors of cardamom and pistachios, which are combined in a creamy and indulgent pudding. The use of almond milk and natural sweeteners makes this a great option for people with diabetes, as it is low in carbohydrates and free of refined sugars. The dessert is easy to prepare and perfect for a light and refreshing ending to any meal.

PANCAKES

Ingredients:

- 1 cup almond flour
- 2 tablespoons coconut flour
- 2 tablespoons granulated sweetener (such as erythritol or stevia)
- 1/2 teaspoon baking powder
- 1/4 teaspoon baking soda
- 1/4 teaspoon salt
- 3 large eggs
- 1/2 cup unsweetened almond milk
- 2 tablespoons melted unsalted butter or coconut oil
- 1 teaspoon vanilla extract

Instructions:

1. Preheat a non-stick griddle or pan over medium heat.
2. In a mixing bowl, whisk together almond flour, coconut flour, sweetener, baking powder, baking soda, and salt until well combined.
3. In a separate mixing bowl, whisk together eggs, almond milk, melted butter or coconut oil, and vanilla extract.
4. Add the wet ingredients to the dry ingredients and stir until smooth and well combined.
5. Grease the preheated griddle or pan with cooking spray or butter.
6. Use a 1/4 cup measuring cup to scoop the pancake batter onto the griddle or pan.
7. Cook for 2-3 minutes on one side, until bubbles begin to appear on the surface.
8. Flip the pancake and cook for an additional 1-2 minutes on the other side.
9. Repeat until all the batter is used up, greasing the griddle or pan as needed.
10. Serve the pancakes warm with your favorite toppings, such as fresh berries, sugar-free syrup, or whipped cream.

Enjoy your delicious and diabetic-friendly pancakes! This uses a combination of almond flour and coconut flour, which are low in carbohydrates and high in healthy fats and fiber. The natural sweeteners and absence of refined sugar make these pancakes a healthy alternative to traditional pancakes. You can also add some cinnamon or nutmeg to the batter to give them an extra flavor boost.

CRÈME BRÛLÉE FROM PARIS:

Ingredients:

- 1 cup heavy cream
- 1 cup unsweetened almond milk
- 1 tsp vanilla extract
- 6 egg yolks
- 1/4 cup erythritol or other sugar substitute
- 1/4 cup Swerve Brown or other brown sugar substitute
- 6 tsp granulated sugar substitute, such as monk fruit or stevia

Instructions:

1. Preheat the oven to 325°F (163°C).
2. In a medium saucepan, combine the heavy cream, almond milk, and vanilla extract over medium heat. Bring to a simmer and then remove from heat.
3. In a mixing bowl, whisk together the egg yolks, erythritol, and Swerve Brown until smooth.
4. Slowly pour the cream mixture into the egg mixture, whisking constantly to prevent the eggs from curdling.
5. Pour the custard mixture into 6 ramekins or custard cups.
6. Place the ramekins in a baking dish and add enough hot water to the dish to come halfway up the sides of the ramekins.
7. Bake the custards for 40 to 45 minutes, or until they are set but still slightly jiggly in the center.
8. Remove the custards from the oven and let them cool to room temperature. Then, chill them in the refrigerator for at least 2 hours, or until ready to serve.
9. Before serving, sprinkle each custard with 1 teaspoon of granulated sugar substitute. Use a kitchen torch or broiler to caramelize the sugar until it forms a crisp, golden brown crust.
10. Serve immediately and enjoy your Parisian-inspired diabetic-friendly crème brûlée.

Note: This is inspired by the classic French dessert, crème brûlée, which originated in Paris. By using sugar substitutes and almond milk instead of heavy cream, this version of the dessert is much lower in carbohydrates and better suited for those with diabetes or who are watching their sugar intake.

NO-BAKE CHOCOLATE AVOCADO TART

Ingredients:

For the crust:

- 1 cup almond flour
- 1/4 cup unsweetened cocoa powder
- 1/4 cup melted coconut oil
- 1 tablespoon honey or maple syrup (optional)

For the filling:

- 2 ripe avocados, peeled and pitted
- 1/2 cup unsweetened cocoa powder
- 1/2 cup coconut cream
- 1/4 cup honey or maple syrup
- 1 teaspoon vanilla extract
- 1/4 teaspoon salt

Instructions:

1. To make the crust, combine almond flour, cocoa powder, melted coconut oil, and honey/maple syrup (if using) in a bowl. Mix well until the mixture comes together to form a dough.

2. Press the dough evenly into a 9-inch tart pan with a removable bottom. Chill in the refrigerator for at least 30 minutes.

3. To make the filling, place the avocado flesh, cocoa powder, coconut cream, honey/maple syrup, vanilla extract, and salt in a blender or food processor. Blend until smooth and creamy.

4. Pour the filling into the chilled crust and spread it evenly. Chill the tart in the refrigerator for at least 2 hours or until firm.

5. Serve the tart chilled, topped with fresh berries or chopped nuts, if desired.

6. This no-bake chocolate avocado tart is a rich and indulgent dessert that is also healthy and diabetes-friendly. The avocado adds creaminess and healthy fats, while the cocoa powder provides a chocolatey flavor without the added sugar. Enjoy!

ALMOND FLOUR
BLUEBERRY MUFFINS

Ingredients:

- 2 cups almond flour
- 1/2 teaspoon baking powder
- 1/4 teaspoon salt
- 1/4 cup melted coconut oil
- 1/4 cup honey or maple syrup
- 3 eggs
- 1 teaspoon vanilla extract
- 1 cup fresh or frozen blueberries

Instructions:

1. Preheat the oven to 350°F (175°C). Line a muffin tin with paper liners or grease with cooking spray.
2. In a large bowl, whisk together almond flour, baking powder, and salt.
3. In a separate bowl, whisk together melted coconut oil, honey/maple syrup, eggs, and vanilla extract.
4. Add the wet ingredients to the dry ingredients and stir until well combined.
5. Gently fold in the blueberries.
6. Divide the batter evenly among the muffin cups.
7. Bake for 20-25 minutes or until a toothpick inserted into the center of a muffin comes out clean.
8. Allow the muffins to cool for a few minutes in the pan, then transfer to a wire rack to cool completely.

These almond flour blueberry muffins are a delicious and healthy treat that's perfect for breakfast or dessert. The almond flour provides a nutty flavor and a dose of healthy fats, while the blueberries add natural sweetness and antioxidants. Enjoy these muffins with a cup of coffee or tea for a satisfying and guilt-free treat!

CHAI SPICE POACHED PEARS

Ingredients:

- 4 pears, peeled and cored
- 2 cups water
- 2 chai tea bags
- 1/2 cup granulated sweetener (such as erythritol or stevia)
- 1/2 teaspoon ground cinnamon
- 1/2 teaspoon ground ginger
- 1/4 teaspoon ground cardamom
- 1/4 teaspoon ground cloves
- 1/2 teaspoon vanilla extract
- Optional toppings: whipped cream, chopped nuts

Instructions:

1. In a medium pot, bring water, tea bags, sweetener, and spices to a boil. Reduce heat and let it simmer for 5 minutes.
2. Add the pears to the pot, making sure they are fully submerged in the liquid. Cover the pot and simmer for 20-25 minutes, or until the pears are tender.
3. Remove the pears from the pot and place them in a serving dish. Set aside.
4. Increase heat to high and reduce the liquid in the pot by half, stirring occasionally.
5. Remove the pot from heat and stir in vanilla extract.
6. Pour the reduced liquid over the pears in the serving dish.
7. Optional: Top with whipped cream and chopped nuts before serving.

Enjoy the unique and delicious flavors of chai spice poached pears! This is a great way to enjoy the natural sweetness of pears while adding some extra spice and warmth to your dessert. The use of natural sweeteners and spices ensures that this dessert is low in carbohydrates and free of refined sugars. You can also experiment with different types of tea and spices to create your own unique flavor combinations.

MATCHA GREEN TEA CHIA SEED PUDDING

Ingredients:

- 1 cup unsweetened almond milk
- 1/4 cup chia seeds
- 1 tablespoon matcha green tea powder
- 1 tablespoon granulated sweetener (such as erythritol or stevia)
- 1/2 teaspoon vanilla extract
- Optional toppings: fresh berries, unsweetened coconut flakes, chopped nuts

Instructions:

1. In a bowl, whisk together almond milk, matcha powder, sweetener, and vanilla extract until fully combined.
2. Add chia seeds and whisk until evenly distributed.
3. Cover the bowl and refrigerate for at least 4 hours, or overnight.
4. When ready to serve, divide the pudding into individual cups or bowls.
5. **Optional:** top with fresh berries, unsweetened coconut flakes, or chopped nuts before serving.

Enjoy the unique and delicious flavors of matcha green tea chia seed pudding! This is a great way to enjoy a healthy and flavorful dessert. Matcha green tea is high in antioxidants and chia seeds are a great source of fiber and healthy fats. The use of natural sweeteners ensures that this dessert is low in carbohydrates and free of refined sugars. You can also experiment with different toppings to create your own unique flavor combinations.

BAKED APPLE CHIPS

Ingredients:

- 2 medium-sized apples
- 1 teaspoon cinnamon
- 1 teaspoon granulated sweetener (such as erythritol or stevia)
- Cooking spray

Instructions:

1. Preheat the oven to 200°F (95°C).
2. Wash and slice the apples thinly, about 1/8 inch thick.
3. In a small bowl, mix together cinnamon and sweetener.
4. Place the sliced apples in a single layer on a baking sheet that has been coated with cooking spray.
5. Sprinkle the cinnamon-sweetener mixture over the apple slices.
6. Bake for 2 hours, or until the chips are crispy and golden brown.
7. Allow the apple chips to cool before serving.

These baked apple chips are a delicious and healthy dessert option for those with diabetes. They are low in calories, high in fiber, and have no added sugars. The cinnamon-sweetener mixture adds a natural sweetness to the apples and the baking process gives them a crispy texture. These chips can be stored in an airtight container for up to a week, making them a great option for a snack or dessert on the go.

SWEET POTATO BROWNIES

Ingredients:

- 2 medium sweet potatoes, peeled and mashed
- 1/2 cup almond flour
- 1/4 cup cocoa powder
- 1/4 cup granulated sweetener (such as erythritol or stevia)
- 2 eggs
- 1/4 cup unsweetened almond milk
- 1 teaspoon vanilla extract
- 1/2 teaspoon baking powder
- Pinch of salt

Instructions:

1. Preheat the oven to 350°F (175°C).
2. In a mixing bowl, combine mashed sweet potatoes, almond flour, cocoa powder, sweetener, eggs, almond milk, vanilla extract, baking powder, and salt. Mix well until a smooth batter is formed.
3. Pour the batter into a greased 8x8 inch baking dish.
4. Bake for 25-30 minutes, or until a toothpick inserted into the center comes out clean.
5. Allow the brownies to cool before slicing into 9 squares.
6. **Optional:** top with chopped nuts or unsweetened coconut flakes before serving.

These sweet potato brownies are a delicious and nutritious dessert option for those with diabetes. The use of almond flour and natural sweeteners makes them low in carbohydrates and free of refined sugars. The mashed sweet potatoes provide a natural sweetness and moisture to the brownies, making them dense and fudgy. The addition of cocoa powder gives them a rich chocolatey flavor that will satisfy any sweet tooth. Enjoy these guilt-free brownies as a dessert or snack anytime!

FRENCH TOAST

Ingredients:

- 4 slices whole wheat bread
- 2 eggs
- 1/2 cup unsweetened almond milk
- 1/2 teaspoon vanilla extract
- 1/4 teaspoon ground cinnamon
- Cooking spray

Instructions:

1. Preheat a non-stick skillet over medium heat.
2. In a shallow dish, whisk together the eggs, almond milk, vanilla extract, and ground cinnamon.
3. Dip each slice of bread into the egg mixture, making sure to coat both sides evenly.
4. Spray the skillet with cooking spray and add the bread slices to the pan.
5. Cook the French toast for 2-3 minutes on each side, until golden brown.

Serve the French toast warm with sugar-free maple syrup or fresh berries.

Enjoy your delicious and diabetic-friendly French toast!

Printed in Great Britain
by Amazon

38691861R00064